Editorial Niches

Editorial Niches

A Companion to

Editing Canadian English, 3rd edition

EDITORS
CANADA

Editors' Association of Canada

Editorial Niches: A Companion to Editing Canadian English, 3rd edition
© 2015 by The Editors' Association of Canada/Association canadienne
des réviseurs.

Cover design: Nancy Paillé
Interior layout: Nancy Paillé, Audrey Wells and Carmen Siu

Editors' Association of Canada
505–27 Carlton Street
Toronto, ON M5B 1L2

editors.ca

Library and Archives Canada Cataloguing in Publication

Editorial niches : a companion to Editing Canadian English,
3rd edition / Editors' Association of Canada.

Includes bibliographical references.

Supplement to: Editing Canadian English.

ISBN 978-1-987998-00-9 (paperback)

1. English language--Canada. 2. English language--Rhetoric.
3. Canadianisms (English). 4. Editing--Handbooks, manuals, etc.
I. Editors' Association of Canada, issuing body

PE3227.E35 2015 Suppl.   427'.971   C2015-903505-8

ISBN: 978-1-987998-00-9

Printed and bound in Canada

6 5 4   22 21 20

Prepared for the

Editors' Association of Canada /
Association canadienne des réviseurs

Managing editor: Anne Louise Mahoney
Copy editor: Shaun Oakey

Julia Aitken
Stan Backs
Christa Bedwin
Anne Brennan
Kevin Burns
Laura Byrne Paquet
Emily Dockrill Jones
Janice Dyer
Glen Ellis
Marie-Lynn Hammond
Lenore Hietkamp
Caroline Kaiser
Veronika Klaptocz
Alison Kooistra
Krysia Lear
Mary Rose MacLachlan
Paul Markowski
Adrienne Montgomerie
Ashley Rayner
Rosemary Shipton
Marion Soublière
Yvonne Van Ruskenveld
Gillian Watts
Moira White

Contents

Acknowledgements

Many people were involved in creating this information-packed volume.

Elizabeth Macfie, Anne Louise Mahoney, Carolyn Pisani, and Karen Virag served as the core team during the initial planning stages of this project. Heather Ebbs later provided helpful guidance and practical help in our time of need.

Stan Backs, Anne Brennan, Noeline Bridge, Laura Byrne Paquet, Janice Dyer, Heather Ebbs, Laura Edlund, Murray McGregor, Mary Newberry, Arlene Prunkl, Jennifer Ralston, Leslie Saffrey, Marion Soublière, Alethea Spiridon Hopson, Gael Spivak, Rachel Stuckey, François Trahan, and Risa Vandersluis offered input on categories and subcategories that proved immensely useful.

Julia Aitken, Stan Backs, Christa Bedwin, Anne Brennan, Kevin Burns, Laura Byrne Paquet, Emily Dockrill Jones, Janice Dyer, Glen Ellis, Marie-Lynn Hammond, Lenore Hietkamp, Caroline Kaiser, Veronika Klaptocz, Alison Kooistra, Krysia Lear, Mary Rose MacLachlan, Paul Markowski, Adrienne Montgomerie, Ashley Rayner, Rosemary Shipton, Marion Soublière, Yvonne Van Ruskenveld, Gillian Watts, and Moira White generously shared their time and expertise through writing about areas of editing at which they excel.

Jonathan Backs, Christa Bedwin, Tammy Burns, Aaron Dalton, Heather Ebbs, Alison Fryer, Douglas Gibson, Anne Godlewski, Tim Green, Jennifer Latham, Paul Ledoux, Jennifer Lum, Brad McRae, Joe Medjuck, Myrtle Moulton, Margaret Shaw, Gael Spivak, Isobel Stephenson, Ty Templeton, and Lucy Waverman provided feedback on particular sections, raising key issues and questions and enriching the text greatly as a result.

Shaun Oakey copy edited every section with grace, flexibility, and good sense, always keeping in mind the needs of the reader. His unflappability and eye for detail are legendary.

Nancy Paillé designed the cover and did the interior layout with efficiency and care. Anne Louise Mahoney reviewed the proofs.

The publications committee wishes to acknowledge the work and dedication of the Editors' Association of Canada (Editors Canada) national office staff throughout this project, especially Carolyn L Burke (executive director), who provided unflagging moral and practical support along with considerable expertise; Grace Cheng Xing, Sébastien Koch, Michelle Ou, and Lianne Zwarenstein were wonderfully helpful and efficient as well. We are also grateful for the encouragement and assistance we received from the national executive council.

Publications committee
Editors' Association of Canada
2015

About *Editorial Niches*

A Companion to *Editing Canadian English*, 3rd edition

Editing Canadian English was written for editors, writers, and everyone who works with words. It presents a flexible but systematic approach to creating workable Canadian styles. The goal is not to impose a uniform Canadian English style but to help editors make informed and appropriate choices for each project, whether it is a textbook, a website, a graphic novel, a scientific journal article, a cookbook, or one of the many other kinds of texts that editors edit.

Editorial Niches began as part of the third edition of *Editing Canadian English*, and indeed is part of the e-book edition. When we realized that the page count of the print edition would be considerably longer than expected, we decided to publish the sections on editorial roles and requirements (chapter 12) and editorial niches (chapter 13) in a companion volume, using the same chapter and section numbering to preserve the link with the print edition. References in this book to sections or paragraphs in *Editing Canadian English* 3 are preceded by "ECE3".

Whereas chapters 1 to 11 are intended for an audience that goes far beyond editors—including writers, translators, teachers, students, librarians, and others—chapters 12 and 13 are primarily aimed at would be, new, and established editors.

Chapter 12 begins with the foundational *Professional Editorial Standards (2016)*, which outlines a range of key editorial roles: the fundamentals of editing and standards for structural editing, stylistic editing, copy editing, and proofreading. Other key roles and requirements discussed in this chapter include professional development, fact checking, indexing, email etiquette, and software for editing.

Chapter 13 is a treasure trove of editorial niches—a rich resource for those who would like to learn more about particular areas of editing before taking the plunge. Written by experts in each area, this chapter is enlightening and informative. Niches include online materials; books; corporations, not-for-profits, associations, and government; educational materials; academic materials; poetry, plays, and screenplays; cookbooks; magazines; science, technology, and medicine; and visual materials.

Whether you are just starting out or are a seasoned editor who is thinking about trying a new area of editing, *Editorial Niches* is a solid source of information that will guide you on your way.

Comments and suggestions

The Editors' Association of Canada welcomes your input for future editions of this book. Please send your comments and suggestions to publications@editors.ca.

12 Editorial Roles and Requirements

12. Editorial Roles and Requirements

Introduction

What is editing?

Editing involves carefully reviewing material before it is published and suggesting or making changes to correct or improve it. The goal of editing is to ensure that the material is consistent and correct and that its content, language, style, and design suit its purpose and meet the needs of its audience.

The editor is an intermediary who must skilfully and tactfully balance the interests of those who have commissioned the work and developed the material and, ultimately, the intended audience(s). The editor is also part of a team that guides a work through its various stages from creation to publication and must be familiar with, and respectful of, the contributions of others. The editor must collaborate effectively with all team members.

What are professional editorial standards?

Professional Editorial Standards (PES) is a vital document for editors in Canada and for the editing profession. The 2009 version of *PES* defined the standards as "the knowledge, skills, and practices most commonly required for editing English-language material." The standards articulated in *PES* are statements about levels of performance that editors aspire to achieve. They clarify what is expected of Canadian editors and define the criteria against which their knowledge, skills, and practice can be measured.

The editor who meets these standards is able to do a professional job with minimum supervision.

Why have professional standards?

The standards defined in *PES* are used by . . .

Editors to
- better understand the range of skills and knowledge they should aspire to
- support their own continuing education and professional development

5

- □ explain what editing is and what editors do
- □ define best practices for doing their work

Employers to
- □ know what to expect from the editors they hire
- □ develop job descriptions
- □ create performance evaluation tools

Clients to
- □ know what to expect from the editors they hire
- □ understand and negotiate editors' services

Educators to
- □ develop editing training courses and programs

Editors Canada to
- □ develop and maintain certification
- □ explain what editors should do when performing various stages of editing
- □ increase awareness of the value of editing
- □ provide products and services to editors throughout their careers
- □ design material, seminars, and courses on editing
- □ support and advance the interests of editors and excellence in editing

Does *PES* cover the entire publishing process?

No. *PES* covers the four stages of editing that begin when the material is more or less complete, and end when it's ready for publication:

- □ structural editing
- □ stylistic editing
- □ copy editing
- □ proofreading

Part A covers the knowledge and practices required of all professional editors, no matter which stages they work on. Parts B through E cover the skills required at each stage.

The standards do not cover other publication stages or tasks, such as writing, developmental editing, indexing, translation, marketing, or project management.

Does *PES* describe all types of editing?

No. Editors work on many subjects and types of publications that require specialized knowledge and skills. For example, medical editors have to know medical terminology, fiction editors must understand character and story arcs, editors of speeches have to be sensitive to rhythm and attention span, and website editors need to be familiar with search engine optimization (SEO) algorithms.

Certain editing jobs often comprise a bundle of standards at different stages of editing. Plain language editing, for example, might include a mix of structural editing (improving organization and content) and stylistic editing (clarifying meaning).

PES does not try to capture all standards that all editors follow all the time. Instead, it captures the core standards—the standards most commonly required.

Does *PES* focus on traditional print publishing?

No. *PES* covers the core standards that all Canadian editors follow, regardless of the type of material they work on or how they edit.

Does every editor use the same terminology?

No. In our quickly evolving field, people who edit use a broad range of terms to describe what they do, the material they work on, and the creators of the original work.

A. The Fundamentals of Editing

Professional editors perform a variety of tasks, from managing an entire publishing process to performing only a specific part of it. Regardless of the extent of their involvement, all editors need to have a broad understanding of various processes and their role within them.

In their work, professional editors should

- demonstrate initiative and flexibility,
- be able to adapt to the needs of the project and the specific work environment,
- communicate clearly and tactfully, and
- respect the opinions of others.

Before undertaking a project, professional editors should ensure that they have the skills, training, and experience necessary to complete the work. Editors should continue to improve and upgrade their knowledge and skills throughout their careers.

The Fundamentals seek to encompass, in general terms, the knowledge (A1 through A6) a professional editor must be equipped with to complete the tasks stated here as fundamental practices of editing (A7 through A12).

For example, in areas such as design and production (A6), the editor may not always have a hands-on role but still needs to know and understand the basic principles and tools to do a proper edit. However, other areas of the editor's knowledge, such as knowing how the scope of a project affects the edit (A3) and knowing the legal and ethical requirements in publishing (A5), may lead directly to the editor's intervention—that is, to applying skills and practices such as revising for style (A8) and flagging copyright violations (A9). These areas of knowledge, therefore, have direct counterparts in some of the practices listed in the second part of this section.

A professional editor meets the following standards.

KNOWLEDGE

A1 Know the publishing process

Know that editors are part of a larger publishing process, whether for print or electronic media. Understand the stages of the process and the roles of the other team members so that the editing work complements the work of the other team members.

- A1.1 Understand the stages of a project, the typical roles and responsibilities of a production team, and the editor's place in the publishing process.

- A1.2 Understand the generally recognized stages of the editorial process and be aware that they may overlap or unfold differently during a given project.

- A1.3 Know the terminology commonly used in editing and publishing.

A1.4 Understand the different types of publications and media and the implications these have for editing and production choices.

A2 Know the importance of the audience and the purpose of the material

Be aware of how the audience and purpose of the material affect the editing and production choices. At every stage, look ahead to the final product.

A3 Know how the scope of a project affects the editorial process

Understand how editing is influenced by the scope of a project: what the project is (its purpose, audience, and medium); the level of editorial intervention required; the time, budget, and other resources available; the roles and responsibilities of the key players in the project; and the lines of authority.

A4 Know the medium

Know the conventional parts of different types of publications and understand their purposes and their usual order or placement (e.g., parts of a book, newsletter, government or corporate report, website, or other electronic publication).

A5 Know the legal and ethical requirements pertaining to publishing

Understand that an editor is part of a process with legal and ethical dimensions.

A5.1 Understand the legal dimensions of the publishing process, including the fundamental concepts of copyright (e.g., ownership of works, public domain, licensing, moral rights), plagiarism, libel, obscenity, privacy protection, and related matters.

A5.2 Understand the ethical dimensions of the publishing process (e.g., the need to address biased, non-inclusive, and offensive material and the need to respect confidentiality and privacy).

A5.3 Understand the editor's roles and responsibilities in these parts of the process and know the importance of addressing any related issues that arise at any stage in the edit.

A5.4 Know when permissions are required.

A6 Know the basic elements of the design and production processes

Be aware of the role an editor plays in the design and production processes and understand the basic principles, conventions, terminology, and tools of that process.

A6.1 Understand how design can be used to convey meaning and to improve readability and accessibility in print and electronic media.

A6.2 Understand how textual elements and the interrelationship between text, format, and design can affect readability and accessibility in print and electronic media.

A6.3 Understand the conventions for displaying tables, figures, graphs, maps, and other visual elements.

A6.4 As the task requires, recognize typographical characteristics, including typographical measures (e.g., pixels, points), text alignment (e.g., indentation, justification), spacing (e.g., letter and line spacing), and typeface (e.g., serif, sans serif, weight, x-height, ascender, descender).

A6.5 As the task requires, be familiar with software commonly used for design, formatting, electronic publishing, and web authoring (e.g., Acrobat, InDesign, LaTeX).

A6.6 As the task requires, be familiar with common visual elements, such as the main graphic formats (e.g., EPS, JPEG, TIFF, PNG) and types of images (e.g., icons, photographs, video excerpts, illustrations).

PRACTICES

A7 Set and maintain a realistic schedule

Set realistic schedules and meet deadlines, whether working, for example, as an editor who sets and maintains a project schedule, as a staff editor who handles one part of a larger schedule, or as a freelance editor who balances the deadlines of various clients.

A8 Define and apply the appropriate editorial intervention

Bearing in mind the scope of the project and your editorial authority, assess the quality of the material and determine the editorial intervention that is appropriate.

A8.1 Determine the extent of the edit to be applied: the stage or stages (structural editing, stylistic editing, copy editing, proofreading) and the level of edit (heavy, light). Use editorial judgment when deciding whether to intervene, leave as is, query, change, or recommend a change.

A8.2 Having determined the extent of the edit, recognize what needs to be changed and edit according to established editing conventions and style, as well as any organizational editorial practices and standards (e.g., controlled language specifications).

A8.3 Ensure that the format is appropriate for the material to best meet the needs of the intended audience, purpose, and medium.

A8.4 Consider the implications of time, cost, production processes, and the intended audience and purpose when suggesting changes. At the earliest opportunity, flag problems that may affect the schedule or budget.

A9 Identify and address legal and ethical problems

Bearing in mind the legal and ethical dimensions of the publishing process, at the earliest possible opportunity, address any related issues that arise.

A9.1 Identify and either resolve or flag possible instances of legal problems (e.g., copyright infringement, plagiarism, libel, obscenity, privacy violations) or ethical problems (e.g., breaches of the requirements for confidentiality and privacy).

A9.2 Identify and either remove, amend, flag, or document potentially biased, non-inclusive, and offensive material (e.g., racist, sexist, culturally stereotyped assumptions or content).

A10 Use common editing resources

Use editing resources, including software and reference materials relevant to editing, competently and efficiently.

A10.1 Use current electronic technology, software, and systems for working with and sharing materials with authors, clients, or team members.

A10.2 Maintain competency in software and software features relevant to editing (e.g., finding and replacing items, marking revisions, and checking consistency, spelling, and language level).

A10.3 Know where to find and how to use current, reliable reference works such as style guides, dictionaries, and databases.

A11 Ensure edits are clearly communicated so that they can be properly applied and captured in the production process

Communicate edits clearly. Manage files and documents methodically.

A11.1 Ensure everyone on the team is aware of the appropriate level of intervention for the edit.

A11.2 Clearly mark and convey changes, suggestions, and directions orally or in writing (e.g., electronic or paper markup, margin notes, emails, assessments).

A11.3 Communicate clearly and tactfully with team members at all stages.

A11.4 As the task requires, keep copies of successive versions, identify who has made the changes, and take steps to ensure that all parties are using the current version of a document.

A11.5 To the extent possible, verify that requested changes have been made correctly and ensure that material approved in preceding stages has not been changed unintentionally.

A12 Introduce no new errors

Make all changes without altering intended meaning or introducing errors.

B. Standards for Structural Editing

Structural editing is assessing and shaping material to improve its organization and content.

A professional structural editor demonstrates a mastery of *Part A: The Fundamentals of Editing* and meets the following standards.

ASSESSMENT

B1 Assess the overall organization and content of the material to determine its suitability for the intended audience, medium, market, and purpose.

ORGANIZATION

B2 Reorganize material to achieve a coherent structure and sequence, a logical progression of ideas, and a narrative or expository flow and shape appropriate to the audience, medium, and purpose, keeping in mind that the medium often determines organization (e.g., the inverted pyramid structure of a news story, the chapter arrangement of a book, the linked structure of a website). If necessary, create a new outline or site map and either follow it or recommend it be followed.

B3 If necessary, recommend headings and navigation aids to clarify or highlight organization of material.

B4 Recommend or implement the most effective positioning of auxiliary textual material (e.g., sidebars and pull quotes).

B5 Determine and either indicate or implement the most effective positioning of all visual elements.

B6   Revise, cut, or expand material, or suggest such changes, to meet length requirements.

CONTENT

B7   Identify and either recommend or make appropriate deletions (e.g., to remove repetitive, irrelevant, or otherwise superfluous material) and additions (e.g., to fill gaps in content or strengthen transitions between sections) in both text and visual elements.

B8   Recognize and either query or resolve instances of questionable accuracy, inadequate research, imbalanced content, and lack of focus.

B9   Recognize and recast material that would be better presented in another form (e.g., number-laden text as a table, descriptive material as a diagram or infographic, a long series of points as a list, a lengthy digression as an appendix).

B10 Select, create, or secure appropriate visual elements (e.g., images, video, figures), if necessary, in keeping with the requirements and constraints of the publication (e.g., budget, schedule, format, medium). Determine the appropriate content and length of captions, titles, and alt text.

B11 Identify, create, or secure appropriate supplementary and reference material (e.g., glossaries, endnotes, links).

B12 If required, create or secure accurate and complete supplemental material (e.g., audio and video, popups, mastheads, front and back material).

B13 Determine whether any permissions are necessary (e.g., for quotations, visual elements, audio). If necessary, obtain these permissions or bring the matter to the attention of the appropriate person.

COMMUNICATION

B14 Communicate clearly and diplomatically with the author or project supervisor to confirm structure, request clarification of content, and propose or negotiate broad editorial changes.

C.   Standards for Stylistic Editing

Stylistic editing is editing to clarify meaning, ensure coherence and flow, and refine the language. Stylistic editing is often done as part of a structural edit or copy edit rather than as a separate step.

A professional stylistic editor demonstrates a mastery of *Part A: The Fundamentals of Editing* and meets the following standards.

CLARITY

C1   Improve paragraph construction to more effectively convey meaning (e.g., divide long or complicated paragraphs into simpler ones, adjust paragraph length for the medium and audience, establish clear topic sentences).

C2   Improve sentence construction to more effectively convey meaning (e.g., divide long or complicated sentences into simpler ones, use subordinate structures for subordinate ideas, choose active voice over passive in most contexts, replace negative constructions with affirmative ones, make non-parallel constructions parallel).

C3   Improve word choice to more effectively convey meaning (e.g., by replacing the general and abstract with the specific and concrete, replacing noun strings and nominalizations, eliminating clichés and euphemisms) where appropriate.

C4   Revise sentences, paragraphs, and passages to resolve ambiguities, ensure logical connections, and clarify the meaning or intention, as appropriate to the material.

C5   In improving a sentence, paragraph, or passage or making it intelligible, change only what is required, while maintaining the authorial voice where appropriate.

C6   Ensure all tables and visual and audio elements are clear and effectively convey the intended meaning.

COHERENCE AND FLOW

C7   Ensure that transitions between sentences and between paragraphs are smooth and support the coherent development of the text as a whole.

C8   Where necessary, reorder elements to ensure coherence (e.g., sentences in a paragraph, bullets in a list, components of a web page).

C9   Adjust the length and structure of sentences and paragraphs to ensure readability, flow, and variety or consistency, as appropriate to the audience and medium.

LANGUAGE

C10 Determine the language and reading level appropriate for the intended audience, medium, and purpose, and edit to establish or maintain that language and level (e.g., by translating jargon into understandable terms, using vocabulary that is suitable to the material, dividing long or complicated sentences into simpler ones).

C11 Establish, or maintain, or enhance tone, mood, style, and authorial voice or level of formality appropriate to the content and for the intended audience, medium, and purpose (e.g., making text more engaging or entertaining).

C12 Eliminate wordiness (e.g., by deleting redundancies, empty phrases, unnecessary modifiers).

COMMUNICATION

C13 When working onscreen, use an agreed-upon system for showing and tracking edits (e.g., track changes, PDF markup tools, revision management systems). When working on paper, mark clearly and use standard editing marks unless another system has been agreed upon.

C14 Use judgment about when to query and when to resolve problems without consultation.

C15 Clearly and diplomatically, request clarification of meaning and intent, explain changes as appropriate, and propose or negotiate significant editorial changes.

D.   Standards for Copy Editing

Copy editing is editing to ensure correctness, accuracy, consistency, and completeness.

A professional copy editor demonstrates a mastery of *Part A: The Fundamentals of Editing* and meets the following standards.

CORRECTNESS

D1 Understand English grammar and correct errors (e.g., lack of subject–verb agreement, misplaced modifiers, incorrect pronoun case).

D2 Understand the principles of punctuation and correct errors (e.g., comma splices, misplaced colons, incorrect apostrophes). Know when exceptions can be made (e.g., in fiction or advertising copy).

D3 Correct errors in spelling (e.g., typographical errors, errors arising from homonyms and similar-sounding words).

D4 Correct errors in usage (e.g., words commonly confused, such as *imply/infer*; incorrect idioms and phrases, such as *hone in*).

ACCURACY

D5 Identify and either correct or query general information that should be checked for accuracy (e.g., historical details, narrative timelines, calculations, quotations, URLs) using standard research methods and tools (e.g., dictionaries, atlases, calculator, search engines).

D6 Review visual material (e.g., labels, cross-references, call-outs on illustrations) and organizational information (e.g., table of contents, menus and links in online documents) to ensure they are accurate and correct, or query as required.

D7 Identify and either correct or query errors in material containing statistics, mathematics, and numerals (e.g., incorrect imperial/metric conversions, incorrect totals in tables).

CONSISTENCY

D8 Identify and consistently apply editorial style (e.g., abbreviations, treatment of numbers, Canadian/British/American spelling, URLs).

D9 Develop a style sheet, or follow one that is provided, to track editorial style and apply it consistently.

D10 Understand methods for documenting sources (e.g., reference list, footnotes, links) and consistently apply an editorial style (e.g., APA, Chicago) appropriate to the material or as directed.

D11 Identify and either query or correct arbitrary and confusing shifts and variations in terminology, logic, and mechanics (e.g., metaphors, characterization, spelling, numbers, abbreviations).

D12 Ensure all tables, visual elements, and multimedia are consistent with surrounding text and are consistently presented (e.g., heading and caption styles, numbering).

D13 Understand the issues related to using other languages, especially French, in an English context (e.g., capitalization, italicization, diacritical marks) and edit for consistency.

COMPLETENESS

D14 Ensure material is complete and, as appropriate, query or supply missing elements (e.g., captions and headings, web links, contact information).

D15 Recognize and flag places where citations are needed (e.g., quotations without a source, unsupported generalizations in academic work, tables that require a data source).

D16 Recognize elements that require copyright acknowledgement and permission to reproduce (e.g., quotations, multimedia, visual elements). If necessary, prepare acknowledgements and obtain permissions or bring the matter to the attention of the appropriate person.

COMMUNICATION

D17 When working onscreen, use an agreed-upon markup system (e.g., track changes, PDF markup tools). When working on paper, mark clearly and use standard copy editing marks unless another system has been agreed upon.

D18 Use judgment about when to query the appropriate person (e.g., author, client, other team member) and when to resolve problems without consultation.

D19 Write clear, coherent, and diplomatic queries and notes for the appropriate person (e.g., author, client, other team members).

E. Standards for Proofreading

Proofreading is examining material after layout or in its final format to correct errors in textual and visual elements.

A professional proofreader demonstrates a mastery of *Part A: The Fundamentals of Editing* and meets the following standards.

GENERAL PRACTICES

E1 Recognize the advantages and disadvantages of various proofreading strategies (e.g., reading onscreen or on paper, reading with a partner, increasing screen magnification) and apply the appropriate strategy for the material and the scope of project.

E2 Adhere to the editorial style sheet for the material and update it, if necessary. If no style sheet is provided, prepare one and update it as proofreading progresses.

E3 In the first round of proofreading, read the material word by word and scrutinize visual elements as the task requires, comparing with previous copy if supplied.

E4 In each subsequent round of proofreading, refrain from reading the entire text (unless instructed to do so) but check that all changes have been made as requested and that they do not introduce new problems (e.g., check line and page breaks, text flow, visual elements, table of contents, navigation bar).

E5 At all proofreading stages, flag or correct egregious errors but refrain from undertaking structural, stylistic, or copy editing tasks unless authorized to do so.

E6 Whenever possible, proofread the material in its intended medium.

ERROR CORRECTION

E7 Understand English spelling, grammar, and punctuation, and correct errors (e.g., lack of subject–verb agreement, misplaced modifiers, incorrect pronoun case) within the limits of the proofreading role.

E8 Ensure that the first proof contains all the copy and any additional elements prepared for layout (e.g., all paragraphs, visual and audio elements, additional textual elements such as captions or acknowledgements).

E9 Flag typographical and formatting errors and irregularities, paying special attention to problematic areas (e.g., wrong font, widows and orphans, ill-fitting text, page breaks, rivers and lakes, non-English words, table and figure formatting).

E10 Check consistency and accuracy of elements in the material (e.g., cross-references, running heads, captions, web page title tags, links, metadata).

E11 Check end-of-line word divisions and mark bad breaks for correction.

E12 Understand design specifications and ensure they have been followed throughout (e.g., alignment, heading styles, line length, space around major elements, rules, image resolution, appearance of links).

JUDGMENT

E13 Recognize and flag matters that may affect later stages of production (e.g., page cross-references; placement of visual elements; alterations that will change layout, indexing, or web navigation).

E14 Query, or correct if authorized to do so, inconsistencies (e.g., in spelling, punctuation, facts, visual elements, navigation elements, metadata, other content that may not appear on a published web page). Use judgment about the degree to which such queries and corrections are called for.

E15 Incorporate alterations from authors and other individuals, using judgment and tact. Where comments conflict, use judgment to mark appropriate alterations.

E16 Choose from among various options the changes at each stage of proofreading that will prove the least costly or the most appropriate, given the production process, schedule, medium, desired quality, and type of publication (e.g., contact information must be corrected but inconsistent capitalization might be left as is).

COMMUNICATION

E17 When working onscreen, use an agreed-upon markup system (e.g., PDF markup tools). When working on paper, mark clearly and use standard proofreading marks unless another system has been agreed upon.

E18 Communicate more detailed instructions to the appropriate person (e.g., designer, project supervisor) as needed for the sake of clarity.

E19 Distinguish between and mark differently printer's, designer's, or programmer's errors and author's or editor's alterations, if requested.

12.2 Professional development

To work in editing and communications, you need a variety of professional skills. If you run an editorial or communications business, you also need a second—or third—set of skills in addition to wordsmithing.

It's vital to stay up to date with evolving technologies and changing standards. Professional development is a continuous process.

12.2.1 Essential skills

The skills required by a professional in the field of written communication fall into three broad categories:

- editorial and communication skills
- technical skills
- business skills

Which of these skills are required on a particular day depends on whether you're a freelance editor, an in-house editor, or a manager.

12.2.1.1 *Editorial and communication skills*

It can take many years to master the skills required to be a good editor. A curious mind and a broad education are a good start. Keeping those skills honed is a lifelong process.

12.2.1.1.1 *Editing standards*

The essential skills that editors need to know and perform are outlined in *Professional Editorial Standards (2016)* (editors.ca/node/11700)—see 12.1. Published by the Editors' Association of Canada (Editors Canada), this document is available both as a set of web pages and as a free download. The standards are updated every few years as technologies and practices change. They cover the fundamentals of editing and the four core areas of editing: structural editing, stylistic editing, copy editing, and proofreading.

Depending on the sector in which they work, editors may need to be adept at developmental editing, production editing, copyright, writing and editing for the web, writing and editing for social media, and more. They should also stay up to date on print and online publishing principles and trends, such as print on demand (POD) and electronic book formats.

12.2.1.1.2 *Plain language*

There is an international movement toward plain language, also known as clear communication (see ECE3, 2.6). Governments around the world are beginning to require that government and legal documents be written so the average person can understand and use them. This is particularly important in populations that don't enjoy high levels of literacy.

Plain language extends beyond wording; it also determines a document's structure and design. Readers must be able to easily find what they need, understand what they find, and use that information right away.

Organizations such as the Plain Language Association International (PLAIN; plainlanguagenetwork.org) and the International Consortium for Clear Communication (IC Clear; icclear.net) are working to increase awareness of plain language. The Canadian Style (click on "Writing Tools" and then "The Canadian Style" at btb.termiumplus.gc.ca) and the Government of the United States (plainlanguage.gov) also offer guidelines for producing documents in plain language.

12.2.1.1.3 Relationships with authors

Editors must be able to communicate clearly, tactfully, and effectively with authors. The editor's job is to make the author look good, and it's critical that the author feels this is what the editor is working toward. The author and the editor need to feel they're on the same side.

The following two books discuss how to work effectively with writers:

An Editor's Guide to Working with Authors, by Barbara Sjoholm (Rainforest Press, 2011), and

The Subversive Copy Editor, by Carol Fisher Saller, a senior editor with *The Chicago Manual of Style* (University of Chicago Press, 2009). (Second edition published in 2016.)

For more on the editor-author relationship, see 13.2.2.

12.2.1.1.4 Research

Editors need good research skills and the ability to think critically. You need to know your way around a library, the archives, the Internet, and human nature.

One of an editor's primary functions is to ensure that the information in a document is accurate and true. This may require you to do web searches, make phone calls, or visit libraries. You should know how to use Boolean operators (and, or, not, and near) to define, widen, or limit a web search. You should also understand how a university library's research databases work.

You also need to know what questions to ask—and, sometimes, whom to ask. Remember that just because something is printed or online doesn't make it true. You need to dig until you find the original source.

Other research skills include finding historical photos, technical illustrations, and other graphics, and getting permission to reproduce them (see ECE3, 10.3.12), and performing search engine optimization on a website so it works well with Google's algorithms and other tools that drive site visitors. All of these tasks require solid research skills.

12.2.1.1.5 Project management

Mid-career or senior editors may need to know how to manage a project. This involves managing a team, workflow, and/or a set of files. It may sometimes be necessary to manage several projects at once.

Project management involves identifying and scheduling tasks so that everyone has something to do, the work flows smoothly from one team member to the next, and the project is completed on time. It's about facilitating processes and mitigating risks. Various types of software are available to help with these tasks. Microsoft Project and Teamwork.com are just two examples.

It's wise to establish a set of file-naming conventions so team members can find files easily and can see at a glance what each file contains. It's also critical to establish procedures for version control. The project manager needs to ensure that just one person works on a file at a time, that that person works on the most recent version of the file, and that no one else can accidentally overwrite the file while it's in use. Software is available to preserve and manage multiple file versions. Some programs also allow users to lock the files they're working on, so no one else can access or overwrite them. Egnyte and the OX App Suite are two examples of software that provides version control and file locking.

12.2.1.2 Technical skills

(a) The industry standard for editing today is Microsoft Word. Editors need to know how to use Word's advanced features, including comments, tracking changes, defining and attaching styles, keyboard shortcuts, split screens, document comparisons, document combinations, the navigation pane, global find and replace, wildcards, macros, page numbers, headers and footers, views, formatting of figures and tables, tables of contents, bookmarks, hyperlinks, page setup, footnotes and endnotes, bibliographies, the Format Painter tool, the Quick Access toolbar, spelling and grammar checks, custom dictionaries, and readability statistics.

(b) Some companies, especially large publishers, have customized add-on tools for Word. Other add-ons have been developed by small companies to aid in editing tasks. One example is PerfectIt, which finds mistakes that Word's spelling and grammar checkers miss, such as inconsistent hyphenation and capitalization, missing or multiple definitions for abbreviations, inconsistent capitalization of headings and bulleted lists, inconsistent punctuation, and international variations in spelling.

(c) For proofreading onscreen, most editors use Adobe's Acrobat Pro. Its sophisticated tools for markup, advanced editing, and comments enable legible, comprehensive communication about needed changes in PDF documents. (Acrobat Reader now includes many of these markup tools.) Some editors like to use tablets such as the Wacom Bamboo to mark up Acrobat files with a stylus. They find this more efficient than using only keyboard and mouse commands.

(d) Some editors use Adobe's InDesign, the industry standard tool for document layout. Most designers don't allow editors to work directly in their files. Instead, they ask editors to make changes using Adobe's InCopy, which allows editors to revise or manipulate the text without altering the rest of the layout.

(e) Most editors should be proficient at using Microsoft Excel. This popular spreadsheet is used for a variety of tasks, from simple project management to timekeeping to tracking permissions for photos and illustrations.

(f) Other technical skills required by editors may include cloud storage and file sharing, file backup systems, computer security, and password management. Those who work with web content also need to understand HTML5, CSS, content management systems (e.g., Drupal, Canvas, Blackboard, WordPress), and other technical tools. Editors who work on electronic books need to know about a variety of technologies for files types and digital rights management (DRM).

(g) And then, of course, there's software for project management, invoicing, income tax, and other functions. Whether working as a freelance editor or in-house, communications professionals need to be proficient with numerous technical systems.

12.2.1.3 *Business skills*

Every editor needs some business skills. You need to know how to estimate the time required to do a job, for example—whether you're doing it for someone else or hiring someone to do it for you. You need to be able to track and manage your time and optimize workflow. You need to be able to differentiate what's important from what's urgent—and to whom. If you're hiring freelancers, you need to understand rates and market conditions.

If you're an independent contractor, you also need to know about marketing, bookkeeping, invoicing, taxes, business licensing, and errors and omissions insurance (see ECE3, 10.1.9). You should have systems in place for managing risk, including automated off-site backup to prevent file loss, multiple computers and redundant systems to prevent business interruption, and secure file sharing and storage. If you have employees, you need to deal with payroll and keep a list of their emergency contacts. If you hire subcontractors, you need to know both the best practices and your legal obligations (see ECE3, 10.1.3).

And finally, you need to know how to plan your exit, so you can retire comfortably.

12.2.2 Finding professional development opportunities

There are many ways to undertake professional development. You can pursue formal education; participate in online learning; attend conferences and seminars; find a mentor or become one yourself; and read and write books, articles, and blogs about editing and communications.

12.2.2.1 Formal education and online learning

A number of universities and colleges throughout Canada offer non-credit certificates and diplomas in editing and communications. Many also offer individual courses through their continuing education departments. You may wish to talk to other editors who have taken a particular program.

A number of universities and colleges also offer online editing courses and programs. A web search for "online editing courses" reveals a range of courses offered across the country.

12.2.2.2 Conferences and seminars

Conferences are a great opportunity for professional development. It can be invigorating to spend a day or two immersed in an atmosphere where everyone is talking about the latest innovations in your field. Whether you're attending conference sessions, giving presentations, networking, following the live Tweeting (or Tweeting yourself), or browsing the vendors' tables, there are plenty of opportunities to learn new skills and make valuable connections.

Editors Canada holds an annual conference that features pre-conference seminars, conference sessions, and networking opportunities.

Editors Canada branches and other organizations offer regular workshops and webinars. Check the Editors Canada branch web pages (editors.ca/branches/index.html) for the latest offerings.

12.2.2.3 Mentoring

Finding a mentor or being a mentor yourself is a gratifying form of professional development. Many established editors are happy to help new editors learn about the profession. Check with your local Editors Canada branch to see if it has an established mentoring program. If not, you might want to contact an editor personally to see if she or he would be interested in being part of a mentoring relationship.

12.2.2.4 Books and other resources

Reading or writing books, articles, and blogs about editing and communications is another great professional development experience. Many editing websites, including that of Editors Canada, provide a list of resources.

Editors Canada also publishes a set of resources called *Meeting Professional Editorial Standards*, which include editing exercises that cover the standards listed in *Professional Editorial Standards (2016)*. Working through these exercises is an excellent form of professional development, allowing you to develop your skills as an editor at your own pace.

12.2.3 Editors Canada certification

One of the best types of professional development for editorial skills is certification by Editors Canada. Even if you never take the certification tests, preparing for them is a wonderful professional development experience.

Editors Canada's certification program identifies editors who are masters of their craft. While other organizations throughout the English-speaking world test for competence or proficiency, only Editors Canada tests for excellence. By passing a rigorous test based on objective standards, an editor can become certified in proofreading, copy editing, stylistic editing, and structural editing. An editor who holds certifications in all four areas is designated a certified professional editor (CPE). Editors Canada maintains an online roster of editors who hold Editors Canada certifications (editors.ca/certified).

Increasingly, Canadian organizations are recognizing the value of Editors Canada certification as proof of editorial excellence. Some organizations now ask for Editors Canada certification or accept it in lieu of work portfolios and in-house tests.

If you're an editor, Editors Canada certification

- helps you identify strengths and fill in gaps in your knowledge and skill sets

- provides professional recognition of your high level of knowledge and skill

- provides a powerful marketing advantage

- allows you to command a higher salary or charge higher fees

- in some cases, allows you to skip time-consuming steps in the process of bidding for a contract or applying for a job

- earns the respect of your peers

- helps raise the profile of editing as a highly skilled profession.

If you hire in-house or contract editors, Editors Canada certification

- allows you to identify potential employees and contractors who meet industry standards for high quality of work

- eliminates the need to test prospective employees or contractors

- offers a marketing advantage ("We use Editors Canada–certified editors, who are masters of their craft").

If you supervise in-house editors, Editors Canada certification

- ensures that your employees meet industry standards for high quality of work

- provides meaningful professional development opportunities.

12.2.3.1 The program and the tests

Editors Canada certification is available to both Editors Canada members and non-members. There are four tests and five credentials. Each test is based on a set of standards delineated in *Professional Editorial Standards (2016)* (editors.ca/node/11700). To earn a credential, you must pass the test indicated in table 12.1. If you pass all four tests, you are entitled to use the designation "certified professional editor" (CPE).

Editors Canada's certification program conforms to international standards for professional certification bodies. This includes a credential maintenance program that assures employers and clients that Editors Canada–certified editors keep their skills and knowledge up to date. Certified editors continue to build their skills and knowledge through professional development activities such as delivering and receiving education and training, volunteering for Editors Canada, and working as professional editors. Credential maintenance also encourages certified editors

29

to contribute to the editing community by sharing their high-level knowledge and skills.

Table 12.1   Editors Canada certification tests

Credential	Test(s)	Standards tested (*PES-2016*)
Certified proofreader	Proofreading	A1 to A12 (The Fundamentals of Editing) E1 to E19 (Standards for Proofreading)
Certified copy editor	Copy editing	A1 to A12 (The Fundamentals of Editing) D1 to D19 (Standards for Copy Editing)
Certified stylistic editor	Stylistic editing	A1 to A12 (The Fundamentals of Editing) C1 to C15 (Standards for Stylistic Editing)
Certified structural editor	Structural editing	A1 to A12 (The Fundamentals of Editing) B1 to B14 (Standards for Structural Editing)
Certified professional editor (CPE)	Proofreading Copy editing Stylistic editing Structural editing	All of the above

Editors Canada certification is currently available only in English. A program for French editors, *Programme d'agrément en révision linguistique*, was launched in the fall of 2015 with an *examen général*, followed in 2016 by an *examen en révision comparative*. Tests are now offered in alternate years. Unlike the English certification program, the French tests measure competence, rather than excellence. Details are at reviseurs.ca/perfectionnement-professionnel/programme-dagrement-en-revision-linguistique.

12.2.3.2 *Deciding when you're ready*

Editors Canada recommends that you have at least five years of full-time professional experience in editing a wide variety of documents before taking a certification test.

You may not work in all four skill areas—proofreading, copy editing, stylistic editing, and structural editing—which means you may not have enough experience to pass all four tests. Be sure your experience is relevant to the test you plan to write. Taking seminars and workshops and practising the different skills may help you to attain the necessary experience.

Be sure your experience includes more than one medium. If you have worked only in magazine publishing, for example, you need to find a way to broaden your knowledge by learning about websites, technical manuals, corporate and government documents, and books, so you won't be at a disadvantage on the tests.

Use the Preparation Checklist on the Editors Canada website to help determine whether you're ready to write one of the tests (editors.ca/certification/preparation.html#checklist).

12.2.3.3 *Preparing to write a test*

Most successful candidates report that they studied and practised intensively for several months leading up to the tests. Simply having worked as an editor for many years may not be enough to enable you to pass a test. The Editors Canada tests are challenging. You must achieve a score of approximately 80 percent to pass.

Before you write a certification test, Editors Canada recommends that you

- study the relevant sections of *Professional Editorial Standards (2016)*

- work carefully through the Editors Canada *Certification Test Preparation Guide*

- work through the Editors Canada *Meeting Professional Editorial Standards* resources

- take courses and workshops, read articles and blogs, and study books on grammar, punctuation, usage, proofreading, editing, and publishing

- upgrade your test-taking skills

- prepare mentally and physically for testing day.

12.2.3.3.1 *Using* Professional Editorial Standards (2016)

This document (editors.ca/node/11700) is divided into five sections:

A. The Fundamentals of Editing

B. Standards for Structural Editing

C. Standards for Stylistic Editing

D. Standards for Copy Editing

E. Standards for Proofreading

Each test includes questions about the fundamentals of editing, as well as questions about the specific area being tested. It's essential that you know—and understand how to implement—these standards. Carefully review them. Identify how each standard does or doesn't relate to your work. This will help you identify gaps in your knowledge and skill set. Be sure you understand what types of tasks are outside the standards being tested—and therefore what you shouldn't do on the test.

12.2.3.3.2 *Using the Editors Canada* Certification Study Guides

There are four Editors Canada *Certification Test Preparation Guides*, one for each test (editors.ca/publications/certification-test-preparation-guides). Each contains a practice test, a detailed answer key and marking guidelines, sample responses by a candidate who has passed the practice test, and sample responses by a candidate who has failed the practice test.

Working through the *Test Preparation Guide* is the best way to review the standards and identify gaps in your knowledge and skills. Be sure to time yourself when you take the practice test. You need to be able to successfully complete a set of tasks within a time limit.

After you've written the practice test, study the answer key. Its detailed marking guidelines offer clues about how the real test will be evaluated. Look carefully at the two sample responses and markers' assessments. You'll learn a lot about what the markers will be looking for on the real test—and what you need to brush up on.

12.2.3.3.3 Using *Meeting Professional Editorial Standards* *and other resources*

Editors Canada offers a four-volume set of exercises called *Meeting Professional Editorial Standards (MPES;* editors.ca /resources/eac_publications/mpes.html*)*. Each volume covers one of the four core areas of *Professional Editorial Standards (2016)*. After you've worked through the *Test Preparation Guide*, work through the *MPES* volume for the test you plan to write. Edit the exercises as you would in a work situation, then check your work against the answer keys. Study the discussions carefully. They'll help you understand how to improve your skills so you can consistently apply the standards.

Once you've identified the areas you need to learn more about, you can choose from a number of study methods.

- **Take Editors Canada seminars and college or university courses.** Look for those that develop the skills specified in *Professional Editorial Standards (2016)*, particularly the ones you need to work on. Past candidates have found courses in grammar and punctuation particularly helpful.

- **Study books about grammar, punctuation, usage, proofreading, editing, and publishing.** The Editors Canada website includes a list of suggested books that candidates have found helpful (editors.ca/node/11738#resources).

- **Review all of the books you plan to use during the test,** and study at least one of the style guides in depth. The Editors Canada website includes a list of the references you are allowed to bring to the test. Examples of style guides include *The Chicago Manual of Style, The Canadian Style, The Canadian Press Stylebook* and its companion, *The Canadian Press Caps and*

Spelling (together, these count as one style guide), *Publication Manual of the American Psychological Association, MLA Handbook for Writers of Research Papers, MLA Style Manual and Guide to Scholarly Publishing, New Oxford Style Manual,* and *The New York Public Library Writer's Guide to Style and Usage.*

- **Find a study partner or join a study group.** It's helpful to meet regularly with colleagues to review and discuss the study materials. You can work on the practice tests and review one another's work, share study resources and tips for improving your test-taking skills, and encourage one another to develop and stick to a solid study plan.

- **Practise marking up text with standard copy editors' or proofreaders' marks.** You'll find them in *The Chicago Manual of Style* and *The Canadian Style.*

- **Write tests and quizzes** on punctuation, grammar, and usage that you find in books and on the Internet.

- **Practise editing and proofreading all kinds of documents.** Set time limits for yourself. You'll have only three hours to write the actual test, so make sure you're good at working carefully and quickly.

- **Practise editing and writing with a pen or pencil.** If you haven't done this for a long time, spend some time getting used to it again. At this time, the tests are all written on paper, so you need to be comfortable writing in longhand. Using a pen or pencil is like any skill. It requires muscle memory and endurance.

- **Review tips and strategies for taking tests.** This is particularly important if you haven't written a test for some time. Past candidates have found it especially helpful to sharpen their strategies for time management.

12.2.3.3.4 *Building your test-taking skills*

Practise the skills that will allow you to quickly and efficiently work through the exam documents. This will help you feel calm and positive as you write the test. These skills include

- skills for writing a test

- mental and emotional preparation

- steps for managing anxiety on exam day.

Editors Canada's Certification website pages include practical strategies for practising each of these skills (editors.ca/node/11738#resources).

12.2.3.4 *Marketing your certifications*

When you've passed one or more Editors Canada certification tests, you've received objective proof that your skills aren't just good—they're excellent. You have a real competitive advantage. Now, what do you do with that proof?

Two things: market your new credentials and raise your rates.

12.2.3.4.1 *Marketing your credentials*

List your certifications on your business card, website, and email signature. Use it in all of your marketing materials. Point out that they are certifications of excellence, held by a select few editors. Display the Editors Canada logo prominently on your website, and link it to Editors Canada (editors.ca).

You must word your credentials precisely as they appear on the certificates you've received from Editors Canada. There are six credentials:

- certified proofreader

- certified copy editor

- certified stylistic editor

- certified structural editor

- certified structural and stylistic editor (offered only in 2008 and 2009)

- certified professional editor (automatically granted to candidates who pass the tests in all four areas)

If you've passed the tests in proofreading, copy editing, stylistic editing, and structural editing, you're entitled to call yourself a certified professional editor and put "CPE" after your name. Only CPEs can put letters after their names, and only CPEs can use the word "professional" to describe their certifications. If you're a certified stylistic editor, for example, you cannot call yourself a "certified professional stylistic editor," and you cannot put "CSE" after your name.

12.2.3.4.2 Raising your rates

Editors Canada certification increases your worth, so set your rates accordingly. You're no longer a junior editor. You're a mid-career or senior professional, and you've proven that you have top-drawer skills.

Whatever you've been charging, try doubling it. Not every client will go for this, especially those you've been working with for a while, but many new clients will. You may have to negotiate, but have a bottom-line rate in mind and stick to it. Some certified editors won't work for less than $50 or $60 an hour. Others charge at least $80 or $100. Consider the sector you work in, and think about what other professionals charge for their services within that sector. If you're asked to edit an annual report for a corporation that pays lawyers $350 an hour, it may be reasonable for you to set your rate at $120 an hour.

To some degree, salary and rates are a state of mind: if you believe you're worth a certain amount, you're more likely to get it. If a potential client won't pay the fee you ask for, you may decide to turn down the work and find another client who will. Your individual circumstances will certainly play a role in the work you accept or decline. However, always keep in mind that Editors Canada certification is the gold standard of editing, and you represent that gold standard. Take pride in this fact, and price your work accordingly.

12.3 Fact checking

Fact checking is the process of confirming that the information in a document is correct. The author, the structural editor, the copy editor, or a fact checker may do the fact checking. In rare instances, the proofreader may do it, but ideally it should be done long before the proofreading stage.

Fact checking is important because mistakes damage the credibility of the author, the editor, the publisher, and anyone else associated with the document. No matter how well argued a document may be—and how grammatically and typographically pristine it is—if it is riddled with factual errors, it will be deemed a failure.

Errors can also lead to complaints and, in rare cases, lawsuits. If the agenda for a conference says the event happens on a Wednesday (when it is actually scheduled for a Tuesday), and the driving directions to the venue say to turn right on Main Street (instead of left), suddenly the conference organizer may be looking at a half-empty auditorium—and your nascent career as a fact checker may come to a screeching halt.

12.3.1 Principles
12.3.1.1 *When do you fact check?*

The best time to fact check is usually between the structural and copy editing stages. During the structural edit, the document may change quite a bit. There is no sense spending a lot of time verifying facts if the text will be cut or new sections will be added.

However, if the structural editor notices egregious factual errors that could significantly affect the content of the document, the fact checking should be done at the structural editing stage so that the author can do any rewriting required.

It is useful to do the fact check before the copy editing stage for two reasons. First, it reduces the likelihood that factual errors will distract the copy editor. Second, if the fact checker discovers serious errors, the author may need to write new text, which should go to the structural editor and back to the fact checker before it goes to the copy editor.

Different organizations have different fact-checking processes. At book publishers and small magazines, the copy editor often does the fact check. Larger magazines may have one or more fact checkers on staff.

12.3.1.2 How do you fact check?

A good first step is to contact the author and gather as much background information as you can. This may include a source list, interview transcripts, reference books, and URLs.

The second step is to go through the document and highlight, electronically or on paper, every fact that needs to be checked. You don't need to check commonly known facts. For instance, you are probably certain that Ottawa is the capital of Canada. However, if you are even slightly in doubt about a fact, highlight it.

There are countless types of facts, but crucial ones include names (personal, company, place, brand, etc.), job titles, dates, addresses, phone numbers, URLs, email addresses, monetary figures, directions, geographic locations, and instructions (such as steps in a do-it-yourself project). If you are very organized, you could flag different types of facts in different colours, so that you can check, for example, all the URLs or all the job titles at once.

You should also flag anything that seems contentious, debatable, or potentially libellous—for instance, a reference to someone as a "terrorist" or a "war criminal." Anything that could leave you or the client open to legal action should be referred to a lawyer. (For more on libel, see ECE3, 10.2.)

12.3.1.3 How much fact checking should you do?

Ideally, you should check every last fact. However, in the real world, that is usually neither practical nor desirable. Time, budgets, and the accessibility of sources may all conspire to limit the extent of fact checking you can do.

At the beginning of the project, ask your client to clarify the type and range of fact checking you should do, and the budget available. Include that definition in your contract or statement of work, if possible. Keep records of conversations and emails with the client that relate to the fact-checking parameters.

If you are concerned that you will not have the time, budget, or latitude to check the document fully, raise your concern with the client. In cases where it seems likely that you will not be able to check the document thoroughly, you may choose to withdraw from the project, change the parameters in your contract or statement of work, or consult with a publishing lawyer. You want to avoid leaving yourself open to the risk of a lawsuit if a serious factual error or libellous statement makes it into print.

12.3.1.4 How are facts corroborated?

You can check many sources to corroborate facts (see 12.3.3). Ideally, you should check each fact with at least two sources. If two or more sources indicate that the fact is incorrect, you should tell the author, citing the sources you've used.

12.3.2 The major classes of facts

12.3.2.1 Biographical information

This category includes basic details such as name, age, date of birth, marital status, family status, work experience, and hometown.

12.3.2.2 Boilerplate information

This often overlooked category includes information that is repeated across multiple documents, such as a tax number, mission statement, disclaimer, or slogan.

12.3.2.3 Corporate information

This category includes details about an organization's headquarters, employees, revenues, and history, among others.

12.3.2.4 Dates

Dates you may need to check include the dates of battles, elections, voyages, and other historical events. Use a perpetual calendar to verify that a specified day of the week is correct. Ensure that an event could have happened on the date given; for example, if the document says someone obtained a licence from a government office on a given date, there may be a problem if the given date was a statutory holiday.

12.3.2.5   Other historical facts

Beyond dates, you should check anything that could be incorrect or anachronistic. Areas to focus on include clothing, food, technology, transportation, prices, and the names of people and places. If a character in a novel set in 1910 is listening to a radio soap opera, that's a problem; commercial radio broadcasting didn't begin until around 1920. Similarly, a reference to Ontario in a document about the 1837 rebellions would be incorrect; much of the area was then known as Upper Canada.

Be particularly careful about facts relating to time and distance. For example, if a character in a novel rides from London to Inverness in a week on horseback in 1800, you will need to find out what sort of roads existed at the time (a rider will make better time on a paved road than a dirt track) and how far a horse can travel in a day before needing to rest.

12.3.2.6   Geographic information

This category includes the names of countries, states, provinces, counties, cities, towns, and villages, as well as of geographic features, such as lakes, rivers, mountains, and oceans. Be particularly careful with relative directions. Is Saskatoon north or south of Regina—or neither?

12.3.2.7   Quotes

If a quote came from an interview, you should check it against an audio or video recording or a transcript of the interview, or contact the person directly, if possible. (If the person asks to change a quote that you have already verified against a recording, check with your client. Some organizations, particularly media outlets, discourage the practice of changing such quotes.)

If the quote comes from a book, movie, or similar source, check it against the original source, if possible. Be particularly skeptical of witty quotes attributed to long-dead celebrities; Mark Twain, Benjamin Franklin, and Oscar Wilde are three often misquoted people. Check not only the source but also the actual wording. Humphrey Bogart does not say "Play it again, Sam," in *Casablanca;* the line is "Play it, Sam," and it is spoken by Ingrid Bergman.

12.3.2.8 Often confused facts

This is an amorphous category, but it includes entities with similar or identical names, such as individuals (Edward Greenspon is a journalist and Edward Greenspan was a lawyer; George H.W. Bush is the father of George W. Bush), groups of people (Senators could refer to politicians or hockey players), place names (Colombia and Columbia), or artistic works (*Sabrina* could refer to a movie made in 1954 or its 1995 remake).

12.3.2.9 Titles

As well as job titles, this category includes the titles of artistic works. Be careful to use the official title rather than a commonly misused one. A song by The Who that many people think is called "Teenage Wasteland" is actually called "Baba O'Riley." Pay particular attention to articles. Is the Shakespeare play *A Winter's Tale* or *The Winter's Tale*?

12.3.2.10 Numbers

Just about any number in a document can and should be checked—it is one of the categories in which errors most commonly occur. Numerical facts to check include temperatures (flag for the author numbers that look like typos in recipes or weather reports that you can't easily check), numbers related to gatherings and organizations (the number of people in a crowd, the number of members on a board of directors), and demographic numbers (the population of a city, the proportion of people with a certain disease). Check metric/imperial conversions: errors in equivalency are common.

12.3.2.11 Mathematics

Mathematical errors could merit an entire chapter, but here are some of the most common things you should verify.

(a) Check numbers in running text against numbers in any accompanying charts, tables, or graphs. Check them against outside sources, too.

(b) Add up numbers in running text. Look for errors such as the following: "The meeting drew 45 participants: 16 parents, 22 students, and 17 teachers."

(c) Check the math in tables (unless the client has specifically instructed you not to do so). In particular, check that negative figures such as deficits have been subtracted from totals, rather than added.

(d) Check percentages. Look for errors such as this: "Of the 50 employees in the division, 10 of them (25 percent) are technicians."

(e) When discussing rates of change, distinguish between percentages and percentage points. For instance, the following sentence is incorrect (or, at the very least, incomplete): "Revenues dropped by 17 percent in the third quarter; 8 percent of the decrease was due to poor market conditions in China, while 9 percent of the decrease was due to a monsoon in Bangladesh." The correct version would either refer to **8 percentage points** and **9 percentage points**, or tell readers the reason for the other 83 percent of the decrease.

(f) Make certain that the author has correctly used terms such as **mean, median, and average**.

(g) Check that multipliers such as **thousands, millions**, and **billions** are correct. For instance, if a table displaying results in thousands of dollars shows that revenues were $1,117.6, make sure the text refers to revenues of $1.1 million and not $1,117.60.

12.3.2.12 Instructions

Depending on your statement of work, you may need to follow instructions step by step to verify them. So you may need to actually make that muffin recipe, build that bird feeder, or reassemble that laptop. More typically, you will be asked to simply flag things that look incorrect so that the author can address them. So if a recipe for 12 muffins calls for 2 tablespoons of baking soda, or those birdhouse instructions mention nails in the supplies list but don't say how you use them, query the author.

Pay particular attention to driving directions. Check street names, turning instructions, and so on against multiple maps. Be careful about relying solely on a single online mapping site; they can be notoriously inaccurate, especially in rural areas and non-industrialized countries.

12.3.2.13 Abbreviations, acronyms, and initialisms

Check that the abbreviation, acronym, or initialism matches the spelled-out version in the text, as it is very easy to transpose letters in these items. So, if the text mentions the Organisation for Economic Co-operation and Development, make sure the short form is OECD and not OCED.

Also, ensure that the spelled-out version is correct. For example, the OECD uses the British spelling, Organisation. Be particularly careful when dealing with the full names of entities that are often known by their short form. It is the Canadian Broadcasting Corporation, for instance, not the "Canadian Broadcasting Company."

12.3.2.14 Text in languages other than English

Check the foreign-language names of organizations that do not have an English translation, such as Société Radio-Canada. Also, check the spellings of foreign words and phrases, such as **à la carte** and **schadenfreude**.

12.3.2.15 Errors of omission

Ensure that lists meant to be definitive do indeed include all the elements they should. For example, the following is incorrect: "In 2015, there were four living former prime ministers of Canada: Joe Clark, John Turner, Brian Mulroney, and Paul Martin." (Kim Campbell and Jean Chrétien were also still living.)

12.3.2.16 Errors of inclusion

Be careful that lists don't include incorrect elements, such as the following: "French is spoken in several European Union countries, including France, Belgium, and Switzerland." (Switzerland is not a member of the EU.)

12.3.2.17 Out-of-date facts

Make sure facts reflect recent elections, births, deaths, and other changes. This is particularly important when working on an update of a previous edition of a work. Don't forget to pay attention to verb tenses. It isn't enough to change a reference to "Prime Minister Pierre Trudeau" to "former prime minister

Pierre Trudeau"; you also have to be sure to say "former prime minister Pierre Trudeau represented the riding of Mount Royal" instead of "represents."

12.3.2.18 Superlatives and other claims

Check any superlatives, such as **highest, lowest, longest, shortest, biggest, smallest,** and so on. Be wary of claims that something is **unique, the best,** or **the only.** Check claims such as **award-winning** and **leader in its class.**

12.3.3 The major classes of sources

12.3.3.1 Printed and online references

- Dictionaries

  As well as general references such as the *Canadian Oxford Dictionary*, there are specialized dictionaries for particular fields, such as food, medicine, and law, and foreign-language dictionaries. Many are available online.

- Encyclopedias

  These range from the general (such as the *Encyclopaedia Britannica*) to the specialized (such as the *Canadian Encyclopedia of Gardening*). It is crucial to rely on the latest available edition. Printed encyclopedias are increasingly rare; the most reliable online versions are usually available only by subscription.

- Maps and atlases

  As well as modern street maps and general atlases, you may need to consult archival maps (showing countries that no longer exist, for instance) and atlases focused on a particular topic (such as *The Atlas of Climate Change*). Natural Resources Canada offers useful, free online resources, including The Atlas of Canada and the Canadian Geographical Names Data Base (nrcan.gc.ca). Websites such as Google Maps and MapQuest can provide good basic information, but facts gleaned from them should be corroborated with other sources.

- Other specialized reference works
  Ask the client or the author for recommendations of works particularly relevant to the text you are fact checking—anything from an academic study of Regency architecture to a field guide to Central American songbirds.

- Photographs
  Photographs—readily available online—are useful for checking visual details, such as physical descriptions of people, buildings, and landscapes. Just be certain that the photograph matches the time period covered in the text you are checking.

- Directories
  As well as general telephone directories, many organizations have searchable online directories of their members or employees. These may also include physical and email addresses, social media contact information, and so on.

- Other online resources
  It is wise to treat many online resources with caution. For example, Wikipedia can be a good starting point, but it is unwise to rely on it exclusively. In general, websites run by recognized institutions are more reliable than those run by individuals. That being said, a number of automated websites can be very helpful. These include timeanddate.com (for the current time in locations around the world, as well as dates in the past and near future), metric-conversions .org (to convert imperial measurements to metric, and vice versa), and the federal government's Termium Plus at btb.termiumplus.gc.ca (to translate between English, French, and—in some cases—Spanish).

12.3.3.2 Organizations

- Corporations
  For facts such as brand names and corporate financial results, your best resource will likely be the relevant company's website or annual report. Be wary of fan sites; the name of a particular Chrysler car is more likely to be correct on Chrysler's website than on a site run by car collectors. If

45

you need information beyond that available on the company website, contact the firm's public affairs, communications, or media relations department.

- Government departments and agencies
Federal, provincial, and municipal governments are good sources of statistics and information on anything from morbidity rates to watersheds. Statistics Canada (statcan.gc.ca) is often a useful place to start.

- Non-governmental organizations
Charities and similar groups can offer useful context on their fields of interest, such as international affairs or the environment. Keep in mind that many non-governmental organizations lobby for a particular cause and may collect or disseminate only information that supports their arguments.

- Professional associations
Associations representing professions, such as the Canadian Medical Association, often keep statistics on their members and provide general information on their fields.

- Music licensing companies
These companies may be able to confirm the name of a song or album, the name of the artist or composer, and the year it was released. (Rights clearance is not generally considered part of the fact-checking process.)

12.3.3.3 People

- People quoted in the piece
Check personal details and quotes with anyone interviewed (see 12.3.2.7). In some cases—such as a personal anecdote dating back years—this person may be the only credible source you can consult.

- Publicists, agents, and official websites
If you are checking facts related to a famous author, actor, singer, or other celebrity, it will be difficult to contact that person directly. A publicist or agent should be able to confirm basic biographical details and may be willing to pass along other questions to his or her client. You can find

publicists and agents through online databases or printed directories at libraries. You can reach most authors through their publisher. Alternatively, a celebrity's official website may be a reliable source of details such as names, tour dates, book titles, and so forth (again, beware of fan sites or crowd-sourced sites, such as the Internet Movie Database).

- Scientists, professors, and other experts
A quick email or phone call to a subject-matter expert can often save you hours of online or library research. Most universities and research institutions have directories of their experts.

12.3.3.4 Institutions

- Museums
Museums are an excellent, reliable source of historical and scientific information. Many have digitized at least parts of their collections, such as photographs, audio recordings, and historical documents. Small museums—for example, institutions focused on a particular person or small town—may be the best source of information on that topic.

- Archives and libraries
You don't need to be an academic working on a dissertation to make use of general and specialized archives and libraries. If you want to ask librarians or archivists for help, however, make sure you leave them enough time to find the information. For instance, archivists at Pier 21 in Halifax can find the names of particular passengers on ship manifests going back decades, but they may need a few weeks to do the research. Alternatively, you may be able to do a substantial amount of library and archival research on your own. Microfilm and microfiche copies of old newspapers, for instance, can be valuable in historical fact checking.

- Colleges and universities
Professors can be useful resources (see 12.3.3.3). Contact the institution's media relations, communications, or public affairs office for help in locating the right person. In addition, academic libraries often have materials that are hard to find elsewhere.

12.4 Indexing

12.4.1 Index basics

Indexes function as roadmaps for text, whether they are in the back of a book, in a cumulative index for a journal, or on a website. An index summarizes the text with a series of key words and phrases that the reader is likely to search for, adding metaphorical signposts to guide the user to other, possibly more relevant terms and other helpful parts of the text. Indexers try to interpret text from the reader's point of view, thus acting as mediators between author and audience.

Theoretically, anyone can construct an index. However, some people seem better suited to the task, particularly those who enjoy analyzing and categorizing things (which is why librarians often undertake indexing as a second career). Professional indexers have the skills and training to create indexes of all kinds, thereby relieving authors and editors of a sometimes onerous task.

An editor should check a completed index for accuracy of page locators, appropriate alphabetization, spelling and syntactical errors, reading level, and suitable length for the space available. In some cases the author may also review the index and suggest changes or additions. The indexer is the best person to carry out any cuts or additions, as one change may affect other parts of an index in unexpected ways.

12.4.2 Stylistic and structural considerations

Several alternative approaches are possible in the construction of an index, with options that include different layout styles, formatting, and language use, among other considerations.

12.4.2.1 Type of index

There are two main styles of indexes: run-in and indented.

(a) Each run-in entry is set up as a separate paragraph, with the subentries separated by semicolons. This space-saving but less user-friendly option is preferred by academic presses, whose concern is more with content and less with ease of navigation.

(b) In an indented index, each entry and subentry has its own line, with the main entry at the margin and subentries indented below it. This style of index is preferred by trade and educational publishers, whose main concern is helping readers find information quickly and easily.

12.4.2.2 Embedded index

Some digital texts contain embedded indexes. These use hyperlinks from an index page to take the reader directly to the paragraph where the information may be found. This format does not deal well with larger concepts that may cover a range of pages, but makers of publishing software, ebook creators, and indexers around the world are working together to improve the methodology.

12.4.2.3 Sorting

Indexes are generally sorted alphabetically, but there is more than one approach. The two most common sorts are

- letter by letter, which ignores word breaks (e.g., **Newark, New Delhi, Newfoundland, New York**), and

- word by word, which considers only the first word of compounds (e.g., **New Delhi, New York, Newark, Newfoundland**).

Word by word, also used in phonebooks, is often preferred for beginning readers and those for whom English is a second language. Dictionaries generally use letter-by-letter sorting.

12.4.2.4 Syntax

An important consideration in writing index entries is their syntax. Styles vary over time and across cultures. Some are elegant (**indexing, eccentricities of**), some conversational (**indexing, a field beset with challenges**), and some may be terse (**indexing, history**), but what's important is that the entries clearly point the way to the information the reader is seeking. Consistency of syntax is one way to improve readability.

Indexers are often tempted to editorialize, but they must restrain themselves. Whether or not they agree with the author's arguments, they must remain as neutral as possible. The terminology of the index should reflect the language of the text, using the author's preferred terms and, with the expected audience in mind, synonyms and alternative expressions to guide readers to those terms.

12.4.3 The language of indexes

Indexes are as much exercises in creative writing as they are reference tools, involving thoughtful word choices and phrase construction and a clear understanding of the users' points of view.

12.4.3.1 Indexes in translations

Because Canada is officially a bilingual and multicultural country, works are sometimes produced in two or more languages. It is preferable for the indexer to be a native speaker of the language used in the text and for a new index to be created for each language, rather than trying to translate an existing index. Ways of conceptualizing information differ from language to language, much as their ways of expressing ideas differ; an index adapted from one language to fit text from another is far less effective than one created from scratch.

Not all language groups are as keen on indexes as English-speakers are. Until very recently it was not at all unusual to find serious academic works from France, for example, that were not indexed at all. Much depends on historical tradition, and also upon the structure of a language. Character-based languages such as Chinese, for example, with its thousands of ideograms, pose huge challenges to conventional alphabetical approaches. However, global communications and the vast quantity of material on the Internet are creating a push for worldwide standards in this area.

12.4.3.2 Variations in terminology

Particularly Canadian concerns include alternative names for First Nations and other indigenous groups; differing terms for the various provincial and territorial legislatures and their members; titled historical figures who may be better known by their given names; and the changing titles, unit names, and classifications that characterize Canada's military history. More generic concerns include women's birth names versus their married ones; the variable roles and titles of persons indexed; name and terminology changes over time; initialisms and acronyms; and synonyms of all kinds.

12.4.3.3 *Specialized terminology*

Unlike editing, indexing is less concerned about the use of specialized terminology or jargon. This is because it's the words in the text that form the basis for the index. Some situations do, however, call for thinking about vocabulary. For example, the index of a medical text for the general public may need to add commonly used terms for body parts and health conditions (e.g., **heartbeat, irregular**) in order to lead the reader to an appropriate section that uses more technical terms (**arrhythmia**). And works that may be introducing beginning readers to new information may require simpler vocabulary to direct the reader to more difficult concepts.

12.4.3.4 *Cross-references*

Cross-references are the *See* and *See also* entries that direct the reader to alternative sources of information. *See* references guide the reader to the text's preferred terminology or perhaps to an optional name form (e.g., **Prince Philip.** *See* **Philip, Duke of Edinburgh**). *See also* references expand the user's horizons by suggesting related topics and other useful information (e.g., *See also* **Elizabeth II; Royal Family**).

12.4.4 Software for indexing

The industry standards for creating indexes are Cindex, Macrex, and SKY Index. Indexing specialists will burst into tears if they are asked to use Word's indexing function, which makes possible only the most primitive of indexes. Specialized indexing programs allow sophisticated sorting, tracking, editing, and formatting for export into Word, InDesign, or XML formats. However, it is the skills and experience of the person who is creating the index that are most important—skills such as evaluating concepts, establishing page ranges, creating cross-references, and determining the significance of potential entries in terms of the document as a whole.

12.4.5 Sources of information

Indexers, like editors, benefit from access to reference works to help them come up with appropriate terms. Besides a good thesaurus, these may include specialized dictionaries, encyclopedias, atlases, and scientific or official government taxonomies. Reputable websites relating to the matter discussed in the text are of course invaluable aids when it comes to terminology.

Besides information sources, some specific resources can help with the indexing process. The various national indexing societies have useful websites, operate email discussion and special interest groups, publish technical journals and newsletters, and hold workshops and annual conferences. For beginning indexers, the standard texts of the field are the following:

* the indexing chapter in *The Chicago Manual of Style*

* *Indexing Books*, 2nd ed., by Nancy Mulvany (University of Chicago Press, 2005).

Training in indexing is available primarily through online and correspondence courses: in Canada, through Ryerson University's Chang School of Continuing Studies and Simon Fraser University, and in the United States, through courses offered by the University of California at Berkeley. In addition, training programs are available through the various national indexing societies and from certain individual indexers.

12.5 Email etiquette

Every editing job involves communicating with other people, from authors, clients, and designers to other editors who are senior, junior, or equal to you. Email is often the only way all these people communicate with each other about the project at hand.

Choosing what you say and how to say it is crucial to getting the job done properly and on time. It is worth learning ways to optimize your email interactions and learning how to edit your own emails before hitting Send.

Emails qualify as formal, legal correspondence. When composing an email, carefully consider questions such as the following:

How is the recipient likely to interpret the email and its contents? What are the implications of someone other than the addressee seeing it? Are you committing yourself or your organization to some action?

12.5.1 Basic rules

Follow these basic principles to build excellent email correspondence habits.

(a) Begin your email with a greeting and the recipient's name, spelled correctly. Double check the name spelling before clicking Send.

(b) End your email with "Thank you." Gratitude is an excellent lubricant for fine working relationships of all kinds.

(c) Make sure your subject line accurately conveys the main point of your email; include the name of the project, if appropriate. Emails with vague, outdated, or blank subject lines are more easily overlooked.

(d) Keep it short. Busy people don't have time to read long emails and may often read only what they can see in the preview panes of their email.

- Make sure each sentence contains just one easily digestible idea.
- Put the important ideas at the beginning or end of a paragraph.
- Group like ideas together.

(e) Use a numbered list, numbered paragraphs, or even headings to distinguish questions or separate points or topics. People tend to skim emails. Multiple questions squished into a single long paragraph are more difficult to read and less likely to result in complete answers.

(f) Be specific about your information and the information that you need from your correspondent.

(g) Word your questions so they are easy to answer. The list also takes care of this.

(h) Be cheerful and pleasant. When appropriate, emoticons can lighten up an email full of requests to an already busy person.

(i) Write in a style appropriate to your relationship with the correspondent. A more informal or long-standing relationship, for example, can tolerate a more conversational style. Nevertheless, grammar and punctuation errors reflect poorly on your skills as a professional editor, and text speak and one-letter words (such as "how r u?") are never acceptable in a professional email relationship.

(j) Avoid profanity and off-colour jokes. You never know where your email will end up.

(k) Consider whether you really need a read receipt before requesting one.

12.5.2 Emails to multiple recipients

(a) Think before you copy someone on an email. Copy only people who need to know. Use Reply All and the "CC:" field sparingly.

(b) Put in the "To:" field people you expect to take action on your email. Those to whom you're sending the email just for information purposes must be "CC:" addresses. (And as a recipient, don't launch into action on something for which you're only a "CC:" addressee.)

(c) Be wary of using the "BCC:" field. Not only can it can trigger spam filters, but because recipients can't see who else received the email, they may feel you have something to hide.

(d) Check all the addresses before clicking Send. It's easy to send an email to the wrong person with a similar name.

(e) Identify the addressees by name at the start of the email if there are fewer than three or four of them. If there are more, use an appropriate collective salutation.

12.5.3 Writing to others on a publishing team

Your publishing team may consist of only one other person, your client, or it may involve multiple authors, designers, consultants, production personnel, and managers. No matter who you are writing to—the person in charge or the most junior person on the team—always consider the perspective of your correspondent.

12.5.3.1 *Writing to superiors*

(a) Respect any established hierarchy or protocol. They are established for a purpose and help manage workloads at various levels. For example, if you have been asked to contact the senior editor before contacting the production editor, then do so. Respect that higher-ups may be juggling multiple documents, multiple schedules, multiple budgets, and multiple other editors and authors.

(b) Don't worry about asking too many questions. However, answering numerous emails can eat up a lot of time for the other people. Consider the following strategies:

- Compile your questions into one list, and sit on them as you keep working. Quite often, you may discover the answers to your questions as you go.

- After you have a list with several items on it, ask your project manager or senior editor if you can schedule a phone call or if they prefer to answer by email. Then be focused and ready to take notes during the phone call, or write an email with a focused, clear list of questions. (See 12.5.1.)

12.5.3.2 *Writing to subordinates*

(a) Treat every team member with respect. The person junior to you on this project might be in a position to hire you (or fire you!) on the next project.

(b) Explain requirements and expectations clearly and thoroughly. This requires standing in the less experienced person's shoes and walking through the steps they need to do.

(c) Provide procedures and links to any references subordinates will need for the project. Ask if they understand the processes — for example, how to use the style sheet. Clarifying these details at the beginning will save time later on.

(d) If this is the first time you have worked with a subordinate, have them do a small part of the job and submit it to you for calibration, to make sure they are working to your expectations and to clear up any misunderstandings.

(e) If subordinates seem to send too many emails or lean too heavily on you, explain kindly but firmly what the boundaries are, in terms of both your time and their own independence. You may wish to set up a schedule for answering a list of queries by telephone or ask the person to group queries in a daily email.

12.5.3.3 *Writing to authors*

Praise first! Writing is a creative endeavour, and even if it's dry technical prose, every author will receive constructive criticism more openly if you begin by discussing the things that they did well.

12.5.3.4 *Email forums*

(a) Use your real name, and behave professionally. Assume that your equals, your subordinates, and your future supervisors are all reading your emails.

(b) Speak up! Support others, be polite, and be intelligent. Communities thrive and ideas are spawned by conversation. With email forums and online lists, shared knowledge spreads quickly and is appreciated by many. Contributing to email lists can get you known among your peers, create job opportunities for you, make you friends, and lead to interactions that can improve your day immensely. Positive interactions in the public eye increase your professional reputation.

(c) Avoid negative interactions. That said, it is okay to speak up if you feel one person is injuring another. You may choose to do this off-list, as being involved in negative interactions can damage your reputation and lead to yet more negative interactions. If you must speak about a negative issue, focus on the issue instead of attacking the people involved. If possible, have someone you trust read the email before you post it.

12.5.4 Considerations for negative messages

(a) Be aware that emails qualify as legally admissible documents in court.

(b) Avoid giving bad news or criticism by email. Instead, give it in person (first preference) or by phone. Follow up with an email summary, if appropriate.

(c) If you really must criticize or discuss another person, try to do it by telephone or in person instead of putting it in an easily forwarded email.

12.6 Software for editing

12.6.1 Overview

We all live in a technological world, and editors work in an industry that relies on machines and electronics to accomplish its publishing task. Word processing software, time tracking software, communication programs such as email and social media apps, project management tools, drawing and scanning software, accounting software, and spreadsheets are just some of the applications editors often need to be proficient in.

This section will discuss the software that we need to edit our clients' words. The rapid pace of change means that only a superficial survey could stay accurate between drafting and publication, so our goal is to point you in the right direction.

For reference management software, see ECE3, 9.7.

For software for creating indexes, see 12.4.4.

For software for formatting screenplays, see 13.6.2.3.

12.6.2 Word processing

At a very minimum, an editor of any type needs word processing software. The standard for publishers remains Microsoft Word, but corporations and individuals are successfully using a variety of less expensive and less sophisticated alternatives. Among these are Pages and cloud-based collaborative programs such as Google Docs.

Features essential to effective author-editor communication and editing efficiency include the ability to track changes, to automate routine tasks through the use of macros and alternatives such as autocorrect, and to tag heading levels and other structural features (using styles that easily convert to XML for electronic products such as ebooks).

LaTeX is word processing software that is frequently used in highly math-based industries, especially in higher-education

57

contexts. While it does an excellent job of formatting equations, it lacks most of the essential features that make an editor's work easier. (For more on editing LaTeX, see 13.9.9.)

InCopy, the editorial arm of the layout and design software InDesign, promised to ease production-to-editorial workflows but has had limited uptake. Whether because of the cost, the need for training, or because it does not meet editors' needs is unclear.

Editors should be alert to the exact make and model of the word processing software their clients are using. Although software companies may claim compatibility, there are many layers of incompatibilities and snafus that can get in the way of the editor's customary best practices, or even undo much hard work.

12.6.3 Word add-ins

Add-ins are additional items that you can program or install within MS Word to accomplish editorial tasks with more efficiency, accuracy, and consistency. Several commercial products are available for editors as add-ins to Word. Some are sets of editorial-related macros; others are programs that embed themselves in Word.

12.6.3.1 Word-related macros and add-ins

Macros can be written from scratch, bought from suppliers, or even shared among editors. Computer Tools for Editors (archivepub.co.uk/book.html) is a free ebook by Paul Beverley that is full of macros for all sorts of editorial tasks. These macros can even accomplish complex tasks you may have thought were too sophisticated to automate.

Plug-ins made by other software companies add to the editor's toolbox. The three mentioned here are available separately or as a set from The Editorium (editorium.com/threetools.htm):

PerfectIt is a program that checks Word files for consistent style. This add-in is customizable, so a different style sheet can be applied for each client. Canadian add-ins for this software check for *The Canadian Style* and spelling preferences from the *Canadian Oxford Dictionary* (2nd ed.).

EditTools is a set of macros that help streamline editing, including customizable actions like Never Spell Word, Code Inserter, and Wildcard Find and Replace.

Editor's Toolkit is a collection of plug-ins for Word, such as FileCleaner, NoteStripper, MegaReplacer, and QuarkConverter, that can be run on batches of files as well as individual ones.

12.6.3.2 Math and other equations

Since MS Word does not format equations to standards in related industries, third-party plug-ins are required to make them display properly. These plug-ins appear to be compatible with software used by designers for print products. Creating images of these equations may still be necessary to help them display in onscreen products such as ebooks and websites. (For a discussion of editing equations, see 13.9.5.)

MathType Equation Editor is a common plug-in used by editors of science and math materials and related subject areas. It allows authors and editors to typeset good-quality equations within Word and other word processors as well as HTML and design software.

LaTeX is a more sophisticated program for equation-heavy writing. It is the dominant tool in specialist circles but is quite a bit less user-friendly than Microsoft programs. (For a discussion of editing LaTeX documents, see 13.9.9.)

Publishers in specialized fields such as science and technology now specify the equation software that authors should use in electronically submitted manuscripts.

12.6.3.3 Footnotes and bibliographies

EndNote and NoteStripper are two plug-ins that editors who work with footnotes, citations, and bibliographies swear by. They can be used to fix formatting errors and inconsistencies, convert citations to a preferred style, and change notes to manual or automated at a single click. RefWorks is another citation management program that editors find useful.

For a discussion of reference management software, see ECE3, 9.7.

12.6.4 Proofreading

Whether the end result will be on paper or a screen, "page proofs" remain integral to quality control. Proofreaders, managing editors, authors, and everyone else involved at this stage needs to be able to mark up corrections. PDFs are becoming the standard alternative to paper proofs for several reasons.

- They preserve the final formatting regardless of the user's settings.

- They are not easily altered by the user, thus preserving integrity of the document.

- They can be created from screenshots or "virtual printing" from any software.

- They can be marked up with free software on any computer platform.

- They eliminate the cost and time delays related to transmittal.

- They increase efficiency and accuracy because (a) several sets of markup can be combined at a single click, and (b) they contain quality control features such as the Comments List, which itemizes all markup and can be sorted by person, type, page, time, and more.

The free Adobe Reader and the sophisticated paid versions, Acrobat Standard and Acrobat Pro, contain pencil-like tools and text annotations that editors can use to mark up corrections on PDF proofs, as well as the features noted above. Inexpensive alternatives such as PDFpen and PDF-XChange Viewer are popular among editors who need advanced features such as changing the page content and shrinking the file size without great expense.

13   Editorial Niches

13. Editorial Niches

13.1 Online materials

13.1.1 Overview

The Internet may well be considered the largest publishing house on earth. Unlike traditional publishing houses, however, the World Wide Web doesn't have a style guide or a mandate or a select group of professionals ensuring quality and consistency. Even the technical sophistication that once limited who could post or access online content has given way to the ease of what-you-see-is-what-you-get (WYSIWYG) platforms and nearly ubiquitous Internet access. As a result, the web has become akin to the Wild West—a free-for-all in which anyone can publish anything at any time.

While many worried that online publishing would spell the end of editing as a profession, the last few years have led instead to new opportunities for editors as content creators recognize the need for quality. As with traditional publishing, the ultimate arbiter of success is still the reader, and readers by and large still prefer the well-written (and well-edited) to the alternative.

For a discussion of editing HTML and XML documents, see 13.9.10.

13.1.2 Scanability

The biggest difference between traditional print and contemporary online publishing is not *what* the readers read but rather *how* they read. Studies have shown that people approach online content differently. Rather than reading left to right, top to bottom, and taking in most if not all of the words on a page, as they do with print, readers approaching content on a screen move their eyes in an F pattern—across the top, across the middle, and down the left-hand side—and take in just 20 to 30 percent of the content. Experts call this behaviour scanning, and part of editing material for the web is ensuring its scanability—the ease with which important content can be seen and comprehended during this scan.

13.1.2.1 Chunks

(a) The major elements of scanable text are chunks—pieces of text roughly 75 to 100 words that make a single point and can stand on their own.

A standard web page of 250 to 500 words should consist of three to five chunks, with an introduction of 50 to 100 words providing an overview of the entire page's content.

(b) Each chunk should be preceded by a subheading that informs the reader what the chunk is about. Ideally, this subheading will state the main point made in the chunk.

(c) Like the subheadings, the heading or title of the page should also be informative, telling readers at a glance what the page is about.

13.1.2.2 Lists

(a) Lists also make text more scanable and are particularly non-threatening to readers with low literacy. Whenever possible, groupings of three or more items should be presented in a bulleted or numbered list (bulleted when order is not important; numbered when it is).

(b) Every list should have an introductory sentence followed by a colon, and list items should be grammatically parallel.

(c) Lists should be no more than eight items. The longer the individual items in a list are, the fewer items the list should contain.

(d) Individual items should be a single word or short phrase, taking up no more than about half a line on the screen. No item should ever take up more than two lines.

(e) There should be at least one blank line between the introductory sentence and the first list item, and between the last list item and the next sentence.

(f) Lists should always be indented from both sides, but not too far from the left, as readers scan the left-hand side of the screen and the bullets or numbers should catch their eye.

(g) Generally, capitals and end punctuation are used only if the item itself is a sentence. If the item is an incomplete sentence, beginning words are lowercased and no punctuation is placed at the end of the item.

(h) Lists should not be written and punctuated as if they are a single sentence. This impedes scanability and defeats the purpose of the list.

13.1.2.3   Design features

Whenever possible, editors of online materials should work with site designers to ensure the content is laid out for easy scanning. This includes clear, meaningful, well-placed images; text in a single column; and plenty of white space. For guidelines about working with site designers, see 13.1.6.

13.1.3 Reading level, sentence structure, and word choice

Another difference between print and online publishing is the type of readers each attracts. Whereas print tends to attract more sophisticated readers (even newspapers and other mass-market publications generally target a grade 8 to 10 reading level), websites appeal to even those with low literacy and for whom English is a second language.

13.1.3.1   Reading level

When editing online material for a general audience, aim to ensure a maximum reading level of grade 6 to 8.

For sites with more sophisticated reading audiences (doctors, lawyers, other professionals), reading level should be one to two grade levels below that of comparable print content.

13.1.3.2   Sentence structure

Shorter, simpler sentences are better for scanning.

Break up long or complicated sentences. The rule of thumb for online materials is that sentences should be no more than 20 words and contain no more than two simple clauses.

Avoid complicated sentence constructions like embedded clauses and complex punctuation like semicolons, quotation marks, and brackets or parentheses.

13.1.3.2.1 Punctuation

The rules of punctuation are much looser for onscreen content. Because readers are generally scanning the page and picking out only the information most pertinent to them, simple, straightforward sentences are best.

(a) Avoid semicolons, quotation marks, and brackets or parentheses, and use only those commas necessary for clarity.

(b) Em dashes often replace semicolons. Always place a space on either side of an em dash.

(c) Use bullets or numbers for listed items.

(d) Favour open or closed compounds over hyphenates.

(e) Paraphrase sources whenever possible, and do not use scare quotes (single or double) to indicate non-standard usage.

(f) Recast sentences to avoid use of the solidus or ellipsis if you can. When you do use a solidus or ellipsis, put a space on either side.

(g) Avoid non-standard punctuation such as ampersands, asterisks, and numerical indicators (number, dollar, and percent signs). Use written equivalents in online text. (Tables are an exception, but these, too, should be used sparingly online.)

13.1.3.2.2 The singular "they"

The use of **they**, **them**, and **their(s)** in reference to a gender-neutral singular noun is not only acceptable in web content but actually preferred. However, editors should still endeavour to recast the sentence with a plural noun, or no pronoun, whenever possible (see ECE3, 2.3.2).

13.1.3.3 Word choice

(a) Short, familiar words work best for scanning. Words under three syllables are ideal for low-literacy and ESL readers.

(b) Prefer Germanic words to Latinate ones (e.g., **aware** over "cognizant," **start** over "commence"), but always opt for the more common option (e.g., the Latinate **benefit** over the Germanic "boon").

(c) Avoid jargon, corporate or technical terminology, acronyms, and abbreviations whenever possible. If acronyms or abbreviations are necessary, link them to a glossary or provide a roll-over or pop-up box with a definition for each instance.

(d) When editing for a general audience, avoid idioms, slang, regional expressions, and any non-standard word use.

(e) Use accented letters sparingly. If possible, choose an alternative that doesn't require the accent. Or, if context can be used to distinguish the word without the accent, leave it off.

✓ To apply for this job, forward your resume.

✗ To apply for this job, forward your resumé.

13.1.4 Keywords, links, and search engine optimization

Although issues of layout and language are common to both print and online editing, online content presents an additional dimension for editors to address. Not only do readers approach online content differently (see 13.1.2), they also find and navigate it differently. Online readers use keywords to find content of particular interest to them, and they use links to access and move through that content.

Because there is so much content online, companies like Google help organize it, providing readers with a ranked list of material on any given topic via search engines. Strategic use of keywords and links is a key element of search engine optimization—the process of ensuring that online content appears near the top of a search engine's ranked list, thereby increasing the odds that readers will read it.

13.1.4.1 *Keywords*

(a) Keywords are words or phrases that individuals type into a search engine to find content. Ensure each keyword appears at least once in the text.

(b) Place keywords in the heading (page title) and subheadings when possible, preferably at the beginning where they will stand out during the F-pattern scan (see 13.1.2).

(c) Embed keywords in the text. Make sure they are properly spelled and grammatically correct.

13.1.4.2 *Links*

(a) Links are essential to web content. They are the main tool by which readers navigate the web. Ensure that every web page has at least one link embedded in the content. Ideally, there will be at least one link per chunk.

(b) Use the page title or main topic of the destination page as link text whenever possible.

(c) Never use a URL as link text. Exceptions are small, branded websites, such as writers.ca or salon.com, which are also used as nouns. Even in this case, a better link would be the title or topic of a specific page or article on the site.

> ✓ See <u>what to pay a writer</u> at writers.ca.*

> *Also acceptable:* See what to pay a writer at <u>writers.ca</u>.**

> ✗ See what to pay a writer at <u>http://writers.ca/index.php /component/content/article/80-pwac-resources/76-pwac- resource-what-to-pay-a-writer</u>

*Underlined words represent the words that would be linked online.

**In either of the acceptable cases, the words should link to the URL in the first example.

(d) Keep link text short—generally no more than five or six words—and don't let it break over a line onscreen.

(e) Avoid using "web page" or similar terms in link text, and never, ever use "here" or "click here". If you can't use the title, try to use a keyword from the destination page:

> ✓ Find out what to pay a writer.

> *Also acceptable*: Learn more about <u>writers' fees</u>.*

> ✗ Click here to see what to pay a writer.

> ✗ See what to pay a writer here.

> ✗ Visit the What to Pay a Writer web page for more information.

> **Writers' fees** represents the topic of the web page <u>What to Pay a Writer</u>.

(f) Links should be styled distinctively online. Underlining is the main indicator of a link. In fact, underlining is used online only to indicate links; do not use it for emphasis, titles, etc. However, many websites now use colour instead.

(g) For the most part, link style is left to the designer (see 13.1.6). The key concern for editors of web content is to ensure that links are appropriately marked in the text. This is commonly done by underlining the words to be used as link text and putting the destination URL in square brackets immediately afterward:

> Find out what to pay a writer [http://writers.ca/index .php/component/content/article/80-pwac-resources /76-pwac-resource-what-to-pay-a-writer].

(h) Place links strategically throughout web content to draw the reader's eye and aid in scanability (see 13.1.2). Avoid clumping links together in the text—except in a list of linked items.

13.1.4.3 Search engine optimization

Search engine optimization, or SEO, is a collection of techniques employed to increase a website's visibility in search engines such as Google and Yahoo. While editors of web content need to be aware of how SEO affects the content, actually optimizing content is not a standard editorial task. In fact, there are individuals whose sole focus is SEO, and they often charge quite a hefty price for their expertise. At most, an editor of online content will need to work with an SEO expert or within the guidelines established by that expert when editing online content.

Keywords and links are two major elements of search engine optimization and the ones most likely to require an editor's attention (see 13.1.4.1 and 13.1.4.2).

13.1.5 Websites

(a) Websites are the main component of the Internet. Whereas the term **website** used to refer to anything on the World Wide Web, today it is used mainly for collections of relatively static web pages created and managed by a select individual or group of individuals. This distinguishes the term from **blog, forum, discussion board,** and **social media,** which indicate dynamic sites with user-generated content. (For information on social media, see 13.1.7.)

(b) When editing a website, editors must ensure that the content is scanable (see 13.1.2), the reading and language level are appropriate (see 13.1.3), and the site is optimized for online delivery (see 13.1.4).

(c) Other considerations include the organization of content on the website, the length of each web page on the site, and the usability of site features such as contact forms, integrated e-commerce platforms, or audio/visual components such as music, animations, or videos.

13.1.5.1 *Organization*

(a) Websites are best organized by topic, with broader information on main pages leading to more specific details on subpages. The editor's main concern is that information is easy to find, so the organizing principle of the site should make sense to the reader at a glance. A home furnishing website, for example, might be organized by room.

(b) A secondary concern is that all like pages are visible together, either in the same menu or through links on the main page (or both).

13.1.5.2 *Page length*

Page length will be determined largely by content, but shorter is better. Generally, a web page on a static website should be between 250 and 500 words, though many exceptions can be found.

13.1.5.3 *Features*

Features such as forms, e-commerce elements, and videos are generally the domain of designers and programmers, but website editors working online with the full website (as opposed to in a word processing program with only the written content) should check to make sure these features are displaying and functioning properly for users.

Editors editing only the written content of a website in a word processing program should at least make sure any relevant copy for these features is present and correct. For example, are there directions for filling out the form or completing the purchasing process? Does the content direct readers to these actions?

13.1.5.4 *Blogs or sites with blog components*

Blogs began as online diaries of sorts—the term itself is a shortened conflation of *web log*. Although blogs have since become less personal and more commercial, many of the conventions of the online diary format still exist.

(a) Ensure regular entries—at least once every two weeks but ideally more frequently. Make sure posts are ordered in descending order by date (that is, most recent post first).

(b) Keep entries personal in tone. Use the first person (companies or organizations should use **we**) and create a persona for the blog. (Some blogs may have more than one persona or multiple contributors.)

(c) Include a byline, photo, and short bio with each post, and tie each blog post to its author's other online presences (such as on social media) when possible.

(d) Create a consistent tone, voice, or theme for the blog, and make sure each post fits within this overall structure. (For a discussion of handling multiple authors, see 13.1.5.6.)

(e) Allow flexibility in grammar rules so that posts appear extemporaneous, conversational, and even colloquial. However, still aim to make the copy as correct as possible without seeming overly formal.

13.1.5.5 *Other sites that have regular updates of written material*

Many static websites have elements that are regularly updated, such as blogs, newsfeeds, or promotions. The cardinal rule for any website is that it must be current. In a medium that can be easily updated any time and from virtually anywhere, content that is even so much as an hour out of date is unprofessional.

Ensure dates are displayed prominently on any regularly updated feature. News items should be no more than a week old, and promotions should not be displayed past the date or time they're valid.

13.1.5.6   Single and multiple authors on sites

(a) Often, even if a website represents a single entity such as a company, many authors contribute content. To the reader, though, a website must appear to be a unified whole.

(b) Limit the number of contributors or personae on a blog (if within your purview as editor). Edit posts to create a cohesive tone, voice, or theme for the entire blog.

(c) Ensure that tone and writing style remain consistent across static sites. Style guides can help enforce consistency in spelling and usage (for more on site style guides, see 13.1.5.7), but also review syntax, point of view, diction, and other stylistic elements, imposing consistency whenever possible.

13.1.5.7   Site style guides

Like print publications, most online publications (websites, blogs, news outlets, social media platforms, etc.) have style guides to ensure consistency across their content. Generally, website owners adopt a style guide such as *The Chicago Manual of Style* or *The Associated Press Stylebook* and make modifications based on preferences and web best practices. Yahoo, a major search engine, created a style guide specific to online content, *The Yahoo! Style Guide: The Ultimate Sourcebook for Writing, Editing, and Creating Content for the Digital World.*

13.1.6   Working with site designers

(a) Online, form and content are inextricably linked. How the content is displayed largely determines how well it will be understood, or even whether it will be read at all (see 13.1.2). Ideally, content creators such as writers and editors will work directly with site designers to ensure scanability. However, in many cases, design and content are developed separately, often by two different departments or even two different companies. In this case, editors of online content must ensure that the content clearly communicates design elements such as headings, stylized text, lists, images and interactive or audio/visual features, and links.

(b) HTML tagging determines how content appears online. HTML can be helpful for a website editor to know, but it is not necessary. For most editors of online content, it is sufficient to use the style options provided in the word processing program to indicate various elements (e.g., headings, subheadings, sub-subheadings, bold, italics, bulleted and numbered lists).

(c) Images can be inserted directly in the text, or placeholders can be used. Usually, placeholders are indicated in square brackets with capital letters. They may also be highlighted or put in coloured text so that they stand out to the designer or whoever transfers the text to the online platform. Placeholders are also used for interactive or audio/visual features that cannot be inserted in the word processing program.

> text text text text text
>
> [INSERT VIDEO 1 HERE]
>
> text text text text text

Ensure that placeholders appear at the proper location and correctly identify the feature to be inserted.

(d) Links also need special formatting not provided in word processing programs. Generally, the word or words to be linked are underlined and the destination URL is placed in square brackets immediately afterward (see 13.1.4.2[g]). Again, the pertinent text may be highlighted or put in coloured text so that it stands out to the designer or whoever transfers the text to the online platform.

13.1.7 Social media

"Social media" is the collective term for websites and online communities where users create and share content. Examples include Twitter, Facebook, and Pinterest, among many others. Because of their social nature, these sites don't have a single voice or theme—in fact, the point is to have many disparate voices. Content on these sites is generally unedited, unless users edit their own posts.

As with blogs, companies and organizations are beginning to use social media. In these cases, the same rules of writing and editing apply as with blogs (see 13.1.5.4).

13.2 Books

13.2.1 Production considerations

All the blood, sweat, and tears that go into getting a manuscript just right over weeks or months is much more rewarding once you hold the completed book in your hands. The process of getting it there sometimes begins well before a first draft of the manuscript is submitted and carries through until cartons of the book are delivered to their destination. Print production is basically a left-brain exercise toward the manufacturing and delivery of a physical, sellable product of a creative work.

Production staff get involved right at the beginning of the process, job costing to ensure that the financial viability of the project is in line with the publishing company's business objectives. Costing also serves to establish the physical parameters to which both the editor and designer must adhere in developing the book (see 13.2.1.2).

Once all those parameters are established and communicated, production staff retreat to the shadows for a few weeks until it's time to collect the finished design files. When those files become available, there's a feverish period of making sure the files meet print specifications, preparing the book for the printer, transmitting the necessary files, and coordinating proofing. Only when the proofs are given final approval to run on press can anyone involved in the project rest a little easier.

The print production process is quite involved, full of technical details that can be somewhat intimidating at times, but it's often formulaic and comes as second nature after a while.

13.2.1.1 Scheduling

One of the first parameters to be set for a book is its publication date—that is, when it will be available for sale. This date generally drives the work-back schedule for the project, and production staff work with marketing staff to determine key milestone dates, such as the deadline to have the cover file completed for marketing use and the deadline when files must be submitted to the printer.

The schedule can be further influenced by where the book is going to be printed, and it becomes a game of balancing the manufacturing costs with transport times with transport costs. Traditional trade books that generally have black text throughout are often printed within a reasonable distance of the final delivery destination, since the equipment and process make it fairly cost effective to do so. With a full-colour hardcover picture book or coffee table book, chances are that the manufacturing will be done somewhere like mainland China, Hong Kong, Malaysia, Singapore, or Vietnam, where it's cheaper to produce these kinds of books.

If the book is being printed domestically, there's a window of four to five weeks from when files are submitted to the printer to when the bulk shipment arrives in a warehouse. If the book is being printed overseas, it will likely take around three months. It helps to know these dates if you're working with an author or illustrator who sees the straight road to clear deadlines as more of a meandering path through creative-licence land.

13.2.1.1.1 Deadlines

What exactly is *the* deadline? There are two schools of thought on this, and the bigger the publishing house, the more ambiguous the idea of a deadline can be.

The first school of thought is the concept of the *real* deadline. Production staff love/hate real deadlines. They love them for the simple reason that they're firm deadlines with clear and predictable consequences if they're not met. They hate them for the simple reason that they're firm deadlines with clear and predictable consequences if they're not met—and so can involve much frantic jumping through hoops. Production folks don't like that.

The second school of thought is the concept of *padded* deadlines, and those are generally established by means of a good, old-fashioned game of broken telephone. Production Manager gives Managing Editor a *real* deadline. Managing Editor says, "I'd better bump that up just in case. I know the designer always takes three or four days more, so why not *build it into* the schedule." And so it goes, with the best intentions of avoiding the frantic jumping through hoops. But what you wind up with is an inexact, moving schedule.

As an editor, ask from the outset if there's any wiggle room to the deadline you've been given, just in case. And it wouldn't hurt to ask for the full production schedule, either.

13.2.1.2 The Product

Five basic parameters for editors and designers are set at the beginning of every project: trim size, page count, colour, format, and finishing. All influence both the design of the book and the cost of manufacturing it. (There are more parameters, of course, but they're more of the window-dressing variety.)

13.2.1.2.1 Trim size

The trim size of the book is basically the width and height of the inside pages after they've been bound together and the excess has been trimmed off the edges. It defines the space available on the page to accommodate the content of the book. A printer may tailor the job to a specific press that accommodates a specific paper roll or sheet size to maximize the efficiency of the printing process and minimize the wastage of the paper trimmed off. The more area of the paper that can be covered and the less wastage, the more cost effective the job is for both printer and publisher. (After all, a printing job must be viable for the printer as well.)

If there is a discrepancy between the trim size that was used by production in quoting the job and the trim size that editors or designers used to design the book, there are two options: adjust the trim to match the quoted job, or quote the job again at the trim size used in the design files. In either case, the result is added costs and delays. The editor should periodically confirm the trim size with production staff, and any change to the dimensions of the book should be communicated to said production staff as soon as possible.

13.2.1.2.2 Page count

Printers arrange (or impose) the pages of a book into sections (also called signatures) such that the printed pages can be folded and stacked in the proper sequence. Ordinarily, a final page count should be a multiple of 8, 16, or 32 pages. Although there are a few exceptions, for the most part any other page counts are either impossible or costly to do. This is why there are sometimes a few blank pages at the back of a book.

Page count is another production attribute that determines the amount of paper a printer must use to produce the book, but this has more to do with the volume the printer would order from a mill. The quantity of the books a publisher needs to have produced is the third production attribute that determines the volume of paper that needs to be ordered.

When providing information to production staff for the purpose of quoting a book to be printed, it's best to give a range of page counts that the manuscript may need to fit into. This gives a printer an idea from the outset how much paper and how much press time to book for the job.

Occasionally the page count isn't finalized until the design of the book is completed. Until that point, the quoting done by production is a speculative cost exercise to select the most cost-competitive printer and to provide the publisher with hard costs to establish the business viability of the project. If the page count does change before that point, be sure to communicate it to production staff so that they can finalize the quote specifications before confirming the order with the printer. Once a print job is confirmed, any change to the specs can result in increased costs and delays with the printer.

13.2.1.2.3 Colour

The colour in a book is typically determined by the content and its intended audience. A novel is likely to be printed using only black ink, whereas a children's picture book is almost always full colour. There are a few options in between.

Most presses are built to accommodate multiple colours on the page. The number of colours varies from printer to printer depending on the equipment they have. For the most part, presses have at least four colours: cyan, magenta, yellow, and black (abbreviated CMYK). These are combined in various ratios to achieve a desired colour.

If you look at a printed colour image through a magnifying glass, you will see a multitude of dots. The arrangement of those dots is etched into plates, one for each of the four colours. The combination of colour dots, their densities on a particular element to be printed, and even the shape of the dots all combine to produce a desired colour. Those plates are then mounted onto the press, coated with the ink, and pressed (or offset) onto the paper in sequence one after the other, resulting in the text and images in the desired colours.

The cost associated with adding colours comes from the creation of the additional plates, the ink, and mostly press setup and cleanup. The more colours, the higher the cost.

Sometimes, publishers will want to add a bit of colour, so a book may be produced as a two-colour book. Generally, that means it uses black ink plus what is called a spot ink. That spot ink is usually a pre-blended concoction of cyan, magenta, or yellow for one accent colour to be used throughout the book. Fancier inks, such as neon or metallic, may also be used.

The spot ink will require one additional plate on press, cutting down on material and operational costs at the printer, the savings of which are passed on to the publisher. Books involving spot colours require specific use of colour that a designer would need to be aware of when working on the files.

13.2.1.2.4 Format and finishing

After determining the size of the book, the number of pages, and the colour to be used throughout, the next step is to figure out the binding and finishing that brings it all together. This is as much a process in envisioning a marketable product as it is developing an appropriate reading experience.

Options for bindery are influenced by the audience's intended reading experience. For example, paperback books are generally lighter and more portable. A hardcover book can be more elegant with gift-giving in mind or more durable with heavy use in mind. A spiral-bound book is easier to keep open in the kitchen or the workshop. On top of that, there are marketing flourishes, such as flaps on a paperback or a dust jacket on a hardcover. Maybe it will suit the cover to have gloss lamination, or perhaps matte lamination with some embossing or gold-foil stamping or spot varnish ... the list goes on.

The key is to imagine what the product should look like early on in the development process, likely when considering cover concepts. Production staff can quote anything under the sun to see whether it would be financially viable for the project. Whatever decisions are made must be communicated to production staff to ensure proper steps are taken by designers in preparing their files.

13.2.1.3   *File preparation and the design package*

Designers come in all stripes. There are those with visual acuity and creative talents who come up with works of art on a page. There are those who have mastered the desktop publishing tools, churning out efficient layouts with keen attention to detail and overall in-file tidiness but with less creative flair. And then there are all the designers in between. Editors who contract designers to do the layout and the scope of a project need to be able to choose a designer appropriate to the job at hand.

The key to working with designers is making sure they have all the necessary information about a project from the outset, giving them the opportunity to go over any details that may be challenging or unclear. Production staff can help better define or explain any file parameters to ensure the submitted files will meet the technical requirements of the project as understood by the printer. The adage "An ounce of prevention is worth a pound of cure" comes to mind here.

13.2.1.3.1 *Colour*

Colour reproduction in general is a difficult thing to get quite right, particularly since layout and design is done digitally onscreen using a totally different colour space known as the RGB colour space (red, green, and blue). This colour space is used in the digital capture (scanning or digital photography) of original photos or illustrated art. In a nutshell, colours onscreen or as captured by scanning or digital photography are created through what is called additive colour, combinations of red, green, and blue light that yield different colours. The CMYK colour space, on the other hand, uses what is called subtractive colour in the addition of inks (or pigments or dyes in other media): as colours are added, more light is absorbed and things tend to get darker, ending up with something akin to black.

For print purposes, both designers and production staff must be aware of and work toward the CMYK colour space (see 13.2.1.2.3). All colours in the design files, as well as any images used in the layout, must be defined in that colour space so that printers can create the cyan, magenta, yellow, and black plates that make up the dots that combine into the desired colours. Any other colour space will be flagged by production staff when preflighting the files, and although it can be addressed relatively easily, doing so may cause the colours to shift, having unintended results on press compared to what is seen onscreen. Again, an ounce of prevention here.

Correct colour reproduction has been a challenge in the industry for many years, particularly in magazine printing, so much so that standards have been developed to help mitigate the variation of colour between design, production, and reproduction on press. The standards discuss such things as monitor colour calibration and press colour profiles. It's basically an agreement in principle between all parties that a particular colour is made up of a specific set of ingredients and is represented by specific numbers on various devices under various conditions.

The colour profile of the printer's specific press, which is a file containing the way that press puts the ink ingredients together to make a specific colour, will likely need to be communicated to the designer; the designer can then preview onscreen relatively closely what the colours will look like when reproduced on that press.

13.2.1.3.2 Resolution

Whatever is reproduced on a press, an inkjet printer, or a laser printer is a specific arrangement of dots. These are the dots you end up with. But the question of what dots you *begin* with is a question of resolution. This is something that tends to come up when books are supplied with images that come from someone's point-and-shoot digital camera or their home scanner.

If the resolution is too low, the number of dots to begin with is too low to reproduce properly on press. The printed image will be either blurry or pixelated. Production staff will most certainly ask that a better image be supplied. If there are no better options, then the image will be adjusted to increase its resolution to match the press requirements, but the result will still be inadequate.

13.2.1.3.3 Fonts

Fonts are another somewhat challenging aspect of print production, if not of publishing. Fonts are much like software, in that they require appropriate licensing to be used on a computer with desktop publishing software in the layout and design of a project. There are also specific licensing requirements around the distribution of matter using these fonts, or having it displayed on a website.

It's a complex, costly, and difficult to manage aspect of publishing. Different font creators or vendors have different licensing terms, and publishers need to be diligent in determining what those terms are and whether they're appropriate for their needs or the needs of a given project.

Use of fonts is further complicated in working with freelance design staff, who have their own business needs. Inevitably, when files are transmitted between publishers and designers, so are fonts, and then it gets messy. As an editor who may deal with a freelance designer, be sure to find out what the publishing company's policy is around acquisition and use of fonts and what's expected of freelance designers.

13.2.1.4   More on print production

There's a lot to know about production, and if you wish to dig deeper, consider getting a copy of the quick reference guide *Pocket Pal: The Handy Book of Graphic Arts Production*.

Another great thing to do is to go on a printer tour. The detailed explanations the printer folks give are that much better when you can see the process in action.

13.2.2 The editor-author relationship

People pick up editing skills from formal studies or learning by doing. They hone their skills in many settings: in-house and freelance, in print and online. No matter the editorial setting or the format of the final product, the core skills are essentially the same. They relate to the organization of the content, its tone and vocabulary, its style, how it might be trimmed for space, the deadlines that must be honoured, and, finally, the recognition that as solitary an activity as it is, editing is always a collaborative activity. Various editing handbooks and guides use different terms, but here is a six-point distillation of the basics at the heart of effective editors in their working relationships with authors.

13.2.2.1 Flexibility

Bach's *Goldberg Variations* is a magnificent exploration of a short Aria, disassembled and reassembled through a series of 30 complex variations. Written for the two keyboards of a harpsichord, it's difficult to play on the piano. Editors sit at another kind of keyboard and must feel comfortable with new and shifting themes, and a sometimes bewildering array of technically demanding and surprising variations. Practice helps.

Editors often develop their own main theme, that area of content that becomes their specialty. They develop the background, know the acronyms, and are familiar with all the key authors. Challenging, of course, but relatively familiar. To edit is to know what you do know, respect what you don't know, and mind the gap in between. It takes confidence to risk moving beyond the familiar, but effective editors are intellectually curious and willing to try the untested. Let's call this editorial flexibility. Consider your life as an editor not defined solely by a particular beat but by the consistent and disciplined approach you bring to managing different forms of content that address a wide range of subjects. Maintain flexibility, as the oxymoron goes. Don't turn jobs down automatically if they are not immediately familiar. Try one.

13.2.2.2 Multiple methods

Editing takes many guises, and it's essential that author and editor both know the mode of editing that is being implemented. Editors Canada is precise and distinguishes "structural" from "stylistic" and "copy" editing, but authors tend to glom them all together in a single combined unvoiced expectation, and editors tend to over-deliver. Like puppies eager for a treat, they enthusiastically edit on all fronts from start to finish. In government and business this is called mission creep. They start out with one focus, only to realize as the project concludes that they have unintentionally added another seven elements. Develop your protective Editorial Creep Monitor and "plain language" your way through your explanation for the client of each mode of editing with a direct "what this means is …" and a blunt "what that doesn't mean is …"

Your editing competitors are also your colleagues. It's important to share experiences and insights. Listen and they will tell you that they move easily and frequently through several forms of editing. They'll confirm that an editorial diet that restricts itself to one ingredient is bad for your health. Consider different types of editing challenges.

13.2.2.3 Client relations

In *Anne of Green Gables*, Anne was delighted to learn that "kindred spirits" abounded. Rather than thinking about authors and editors, condescendingly, as students and teachers, place yourself in the Anne camp. Authors and editors are kindred spirits in this together, each with as much to learn from and to offer the other.

Most editors tend to arrive at that first meeting with the author overly aware of what they bring to the relationship: a stylistic safety net, unerring factual correctness, and an often alarming commitment to inexplicable and unbending rules. Authors tend to arrive with a certain awkwardness, if not dread, and sometimes confuse an editor's questions as threatening behaviour intended to humiliate. It is not the editor's job to attempt a life-makeover with an author. Similarly, it is not the author's responsibility to magic their editors into facts-at-the-fingertips content experts. Together, author and editor can create a trusting, professional relationship whereby their collaborative work results in a commercially and critically successful outcome—with on-time payment for the editor and a pristine copy of the published work.

Displaying a respectful understanding of creative collaboration is how effective editors work with authors, and how authors gain confidence during the sometimes bumpy prepublication process. Things become difficult when either party steps into a role that neither appreciates nor expects. During the back-and-forth of the editing process ask your author: "How are we doing? Is this going the way you expected? Is this helping you?" If things are so difficult that you can't ask these simple questions, then you are in really difficult territory, those aching unbridgeable spaces between people that Anton Chekhov captures in his plays in the oft-repeated line, "If you only knew ..." Something in the relationship needs attention. Silence doesn't work. Speak up.

13.2.2.4 *Contracts and letters of agreement*

In the beginning was the word and the word became contractual. Author/editor contracts, like any negotiated arrangements, are the food and water that ensure the working process is well nourished. There are all manner of contractual templates to use or adapt, and one is available on the Editors Canada website (editors.ca/hire/sfea/index.html). Use it, or find another and make it work for you. Every project, from one-offs to sustained long-term arrangements, needs a contractual agreement to keep everything clear. Once signed, these documents often disappear into a large folder rarely to be opened again. When things go wrong editorially they can become very messily wrong very quickly. This is when a contract or a letter of agreement's utility becomes obvious. It allows you to focus on the details of what you promised rather than the emotional overlay of what can feel like a personal disagreement. Most editors approach the work focusing on the quality of the end product and have the capacity to benignly overlook shifting deadlines and altered expectations. Gratitude at finally having that juicy manuscript to savour should not suppress an editor's ability to look at what is in front of them coolly and contractually. A contract is not a restraining order. Think of it as the equivalent of that floor lighting system that guides you to the emergency exits in the unlikely eventuality of ... the editorially unthinkable. You'll feel safer just knowing it's there.

13.2.2.5   *Management of difficult situations*

To paraphrase the opening of *Anna Karenina*, "All happy edits are alike; each unhappy edit is unhappy in its own way." Projects can disintegrate, writers and editor sometimes disappear only to return as unrecognizable shadows of their former reliable selves. Even with a contract in your back pocket, patience, appropriate humour, and buckets of goodwill, some editing projects turn nightmarish. That's when it's time to ask the obvious: "How are we doing now?" "Do you think we ought to make some changes to the way we are doing things?" And most important of all: "Do you want to resolve this?"

Silence and escalating exchanges of emails are the least effective approaches to managing these difficult situations. If in doubt, ask. And in a real conversation, not a Tweet.

13.2.2.6   *Voice respect*

In *Amelia*, Édouard Lock's 2002 ballet for La La La Human Steps, bodies spin dangerously, relying on each other for lift and support. Occasionally, it seems they will fall. Precise choreography and the disciplined skill of each dancer demonstrate danger in real time.

Dance lessons are not essential for editors, but an appreciation of risk and a respect for interdependency certainly are. Editors have the skills to alter any manuscript at the stroke of a key. We can transform it into the kind of work we prefer, even if that may not be the stated intent of the author. It's a constant temptation to impose rather than suggest. Editors notice things unintended by the author. This noticing drives the impulse to tell authors not only what they are trying to say but also how they ought to say it. At the end of every project you should ask the author: "Is this still the work you intended and does it still sound like you?" We should not practise ventriloquism at the expense of our clients. Unless rewriting is specifically in the contract, restraint is called for. An author's voice, like a pianist's touch, a vocalist's timbre, an artist's colour sense, a dancer's poise, is their precious gift. Treat it with respect.

Finally, in *Inside Memory: Pages from a Writer's Workbook*, the late Timothy Findley says that the voice of a work is its all-important "gesture":

> Words in a sentence are a written gesture. And if the cadence is wrong—if the rhythm is wrong—if a single syllable is out of place—the sentence fails ... the book fails. Why? Because you have failed to impel the reader forward with every gesture ... right to the "fingertips"—all the way from the solar plexus. That's where books are written. That's where readers read. ([HarperCollins, 1990], 184; his ellipses)

And that's also where effective editors edit their manuscripts in all manner of ways and for all manner of readers. Try it.

13.2.3 The editing process for non-fiction books

Editing non-fiction books is a collaborative process in which an editor revises a manuscript so it is correct, clear, and consistent and meets the client's goals and needs. The process begins with determining the scope of the project, moves through a series of stages in which you edit and incorporate author or client feedback, and ends with final client sign-off.

In one sense, editing non-fiction books is like editing any other media, because the same principles and procedures are used. Yet it is different because of the length and complexity of books themselves. The length, generally between 70,000 and 100,000 words, means that the editing could take months or even years rather than days. The many elements require the editor to be aware of many standards. As well as a copyright page, a table of contents and chapters, and headers and footers, a book can have quotations, tables, illustrations, captions, photo credit lists, footnotes, endnotes, and appendices. The editor has to focus on the individual parts and make sure the book works as a whole.

13.2.3.1 *Manuscript analysis*

As you open the file for a new project, the temptation is to plunge into editing. But before changing a period or correcting a spelling error, take time to identify the factors that will affect the editing.

13.2.3.1.1 *Purpose of analysis*

A manuscript analysis is not a close read of the book, but a survey that allows you to identify the strengths and challenges of the manuscript, the client's goals and expectations, and the type of editing needed. The results let you know whether you are able to do the work and, in some cases, want to. They also let you figure out the scope of work, the time required, and the estimated cost.

The findings will help you make good decisions during the editing and better manage author and client expectations and communications. They will help the novice author better understand the process, and the discussions may reveal how realistic the client is and how well you can work together.

For a book-length manuscript, one analysis may be enough, but in some cases it's better to divide the task in two. First do a less in-depth analysis to use for your estimate or quotation. This involves looking at the structure and closely at a few pages in the middle to assess language issues. (Don't use the opening chapters because they are usually better than the others.) If you get the job and the book needs a lot of work, do a more in-depth review to identify problems and work out how to solve them. That review would be part of the editing process.

13.2.3.1.2 *Process and checklists*

Some editors can use a mental checklist when surveying a manuscript. Others prefer to use lists like those in the following tables. As you work, keep a record of your findings.

An experienced writer or publisher will readily answer your questions. The less experienced client may need explanations from you in order to tell you what you need to know so you can make informed decisions.

Table 13.1 Client expectations and requirements checklist

Elements	Factors to check	Application
Purpose	To inform, entertain, persuade?	Affects tone, language, structure, and editorial decisions.
Intended reader	Who is primary reader? Others who might be interested in the topic?	
	If a client says "everyone," ask who is most likely to read it?	
Style guide	What will affect style decisions? • English being used (Canadian, U.S., U.K.) • dictionary • existing style guide/publisher's house style • conventions for the subject • author's preferences	Affects editorial decisions and your contribution to the style guide.
Showing revisions and suggestions	What is the client most comfortable with: • track changes and comments, • track changes, with queries embedded in the text, or • changes and explanations shown in the text (e.g., in a different font or highlighted)? Who inputs changes: client or editor? How many passes are expected?	• Affects scheduling, ease of work, costs, and client-editor relations. • Helps in setting priorities.

(continued)

Table 13.1   (continued)

Elements	Factors to check	Application
Budget	How much can the client afford? • Publishers may give you a budget. • Ask independent clients about their budget. The conversation will give you clues about their expectations. • Some clients will ask for an estimate and go from there.	• Affects how much work you can do. • Helps in setting priorities. In discussing costs, talk about the benefits (readability, enhancing author's reputation), as well as the features (the type of editing).
Deadline	What is the deadline for a finished manuscript? Ask independent authors if they need books for a certain date (e.g., a planned launch). When will the client be away and not able to do reviews and answer questions?	Affects scheduling and whether you can take the job. Inexperienced clients may not realize how long production takes and what the schedule needs to be. Affects scheduling and editor's frustration levels.
Publi-cation	How is it being published? • traditional publisher • self-publishing by – organization or company – writer In what format is it being published? • book, ebook, or both? • if a traditional book, what size?	• A publisher and/or an organization may have requirements about style, content, deadlines, and approvals. • Format affects decisions about style, appropriate section length, sidebars, etc.

Table 13.2   Physical specifications checklist

Elements	Factors to check	Application
Length and divisions	Number of words? Chapters? Additional sections? E.g., • reference list • endnotes and/or footnotes • photo credits • resources • cover copy, flap copy	• Affects estimates and schedules. • Checking references and notes can significantly slow the process.
Figures, photos, and tables	Are there figures, photos, and/or tables? If so, ask • how many are there? • will the photos have captions? • who is compiling the lists of credits? • placement—who's doing it? • permissions—who's getting them?	• Checking figures, photographs, and tables and getting permissions can slow the editor's pace. • The editor has to build in time to check that the captions are correct; correlate the lists of credits with the book's contents; check that the placement of figures, tables, and photos is correct.

Table 13.3   Editing indicators checklist

The edits	Factors to check and signs of problems	Application
Genre: e.g., • memoir/ biography • essays • how-to • travel • reference	• Am I familiar with the conventions of this genre? What would I need to learn? • Significant amount of content does not fit the genre, the stated purpose, or the intended readership.	• Different genres have different conventions. • Readers have expectations of different genres that affect editing decisions.
Formatting	• overuse or inappropriate use of bold, italics, heading styles, etc.	• May need to clean up formatting to make the editing easier.
Structural edit	• table of contents is unclear or not in the book; topics appear out of order • significant gaps (e.g., an expected topic is missing) • introduction does not lay a good foundation • chapter or section is under- or overwritten • excessive repetition; lack of necessary information or detail • lack of clear introductions and transitions • lacks logic and clear argumentation • text could fit in a list, text box, or appendix • information is unsafe, illegal, inappropriate (e.g., private information is revealed)	• A book needs a strong framework. You may need to create a table of contents so you have a guide. • Reorganization requires thought, time, and consultation with and approvals from the author and/or client. • If a great deal of structural editing has to be done, plan to hold off on stylistic and copy editing. • A novice author may need coaching (see 13.2.4.1).

(continued)

Table 13.3 (continued)

The edits	Factors to check and signs of problems	Application
Stylistic edit	• inappropriate word choices/awkward sentence construction • inconsistent and/or inappropriate tone • arguments do not make sense, are illogical, or are weak • abstract language; lacks concrete examples, anecdotes, and/or emotive language • sentence style inappropriate for type of book/intended reader	• The style needs to fit the conventions of the genre and reader expectations. • A novice author may need coaching (see 13.2.4.1).
Copy edit	• errors in grammar, punctuation, spelling, usage • inconsistencies • facts are wrong • citations are needed • copyright acknowledgement or permissions are needed	• Check against style guide/conventions. • A novice author may need coaching (see 13.2.4.1). (For fact checking, see 12.3.)
Assembly	Who is assembling the book, doing a final check, and correlating lists with content?	Affects scheduling and costs.

13.2.3.1.3 Scope of work

Prepare a scope of work that summarizes the types of editing needed and an estimate of the cost and time involved. Don't be overly detailed, because the client may be overwhelmed. Work with the client to determine what you will actually be doing.

If a client has stipulated what you are to do, use the analysis to discuss the need for other types of editing and whether the required work can be done within the budget and by the deadline.

13.2.3.2 The editing process

This section provides suggestions on effectively managing the editing process.

For definitions of structural, stylistic, and copy editing, see Editors Canada's *Professional Editorial Standards (2016)* (editors .ca/node/11700).

13.2.3.2.1 Number of passes

Ideally, an editor will do each type of editing separately. Trying to do structural and stylistic and copy editing all in one go is counterproductive. If you look for something specific you'll find it; if you try to look for everything at once, you'll miss obvious errors.

Many editors do the stylistic and copy edits together and then a final copy edit and cleanup. Editors often work section by section or chapter by chapter, and switch from editing new material to revising returned files.

The total number of passes will also depend on the extent of author changes and how often files are exchanged. You may wish to specify a number of editing passes in the estimate or quotation.

13.2.3.2.2 The editing itself

Some editors start with the most complex task first; others like to begin by cleaning up the formatting and fixing errors in mechanics, to reduce visual distractions while they do a structural or stylistic edit. This could involve, for example, changing double spaces to single spaces or changing hyphens to en dashes in number ranges. If the client does not want to see "minor" mechanical changes, switch off track changes before making the changes. Some clients prefer to see a sample chapter with all the changes before agreeing to this method, while others want to see every change. Automate the process when you can. (For word processing software, see 12.6.2.)

Manage risk. Keep track of the project by changing file names to reflect the stage of work (or moving files to folders whose names indicate the stage) and using a tracking system to record the status of the parts of the book. Back up frequently and to external storage such as the cloud or portable media.

Before making structural changes, discuss your recommendations with the client or author. Submit a sample edit of a chapter or section. After receiving approval, go ahead. Be flexible when an author or client does not accept all the revisions. If the author makes extensive changes, you'll have to start fresh. If this extends the time required for the edit and you have defined the scope of work in your estimate or quote, let the client know and negotiate a new fee.

As you edit, be humble as well as confident. Don't, for example, assume that a word or phrase or jargon is wrong. Before you change it, check whether it is accepted in a particular discipline or sector. At the same time, don't assume the author is correct and don't ignore your gut instinct; if you sense something is amiss, check it out.

It can save time and help keep you focused to occasionally stop and take care of repeated mechanical problems, such as an inconsistency in spelling.

After all the chapters have been approved and the illustrations placed, assemble the book. You can use the Outline view in Word to check the structure and level of headings. To correlate lists of figures, illustrations, and acknowledgements with the content, you could open two files or use a split screen or two windows to see both the list and text and use the Navigation pane or Find to move about. The proofreader will check that page numbers are correct.

Do a final check for mechanics and consistency.

13.2.3.2.3 Queries

Editors write comments and queries to flag or explain revisions, to ask for clarification, and to make suggestions. Write your comments simply and with respect. The type and number of queries depends on the author's or publisher's preference and how familiar they are with editing. You don't need to explain standard changes, such as correcting spelling errors. Nor do you have to repeatedly explain the same changes. Instead, explain the revision in a comment at the first occurrence and then use short comments to identify what you have done. Or give detailed explanations the first few times and after that make the changes without commenting on them.

Take time to check your queries for clarity, correctness, and a respectful tone.

13.2.3.2.4 The end

Remember to get a final sign-off. Then store or return the files as required. If you're pleased with the results, use the title in your marketing.

For further reading

Shipton, Rosemary. "Twelve-Step Editing." *The Editors' Weekly*. http://blog.editors.ca/2014/11/twelve-step-editing.

13.2.4 Editing a self-publishing author

An email arrives. "I've just read your profile in the Editors Canada Directory and I'd like you to look at my book. I've got a publishing contract with a company that agreed to print it. It's the story of my family going back to the late 1700s. All it needs is a final once-over. My grandson helped me with the layout template and the photos have turned out very well. My sister-in-law was a teacher and she checked the spelling so it shouldn't take you long."

Bypassing established trades and skills is nothing new. The 1950s saw an unstoppable push toward do-it-yourself, much to the distress of tradespeople who had spent years in rigorous training. Then, a generation later, things turned inward with the arrival of the "self-help" movement, reinforcing the notion that everyone is capable of anything and only negativity holds us back. Editing is art, a craft, and a trade. And today, anyone can assert: "I am an editor"—training and skills notwithstanding.

Today, everyone is a creator, writer, designer, publisher, publicist, and brand. We have the hardware and software at our fingertips, regardless of our capacity to use them. Few editors at work today have escaped the experience of this sidelining of our professional skills. We work amidst a surge toward self-everything, and especially publishing. What follows is intended as a tipsheet for editors when working with clients intent on self-publishing. It's about infiltrating standards that are frequently not understood by self-publishing clients.

13.2.4.1 Working with first-time authors

13.2.4.1.1 Language

One of the greatest challenges for the first-time author is the specific technical language editors use and the generalized understanding of less experienced clients. First-time authors typically think that "editing" means catching typos, and they hire an editor reluctantly, since they are confident *there spell chequer court them awl.*

Many clients embarking on the self-publishing route routinely confuse "print" with "publish." They often believe "edit" concerns only spelling and punctuation. Substantive, content, structure? What's that?

You will need to spell it out. For the editor, each project will entail a mini Editing 101 and Publishing 101 course before you can turn to the specific challenges of the work at hand. Today, self-publishing often encourages a hybrid form of production, one that mixes print and electronic publications. Writing and editing for screen and print publications overlap but are not the same skills. Editors need to spell this out to less-experienced clients.

There is no common understanding of the terms we use, the shifting ground of book production, consumer interest in the content, or the market's preferences for ebooks or printed books. Amidst this uncertainty, as editors we have the role of inspiring confidence in "the work" even as we set about introducing multi-level editorial standards in response to that deeply felt but imprecise request: "Can you fix?" "Will you take a look?" "Is it readable?"

13.2.4.1.2 Blurring the role of the editor

Editors certainly need to inform self-publishing clients about the mechanics and the business of online and in-print publishing, but unless it is a component of the agreement, editors are not the client's literary agent or publishing consultant. As editors, we too must be careful about the shift to "I could do that myself" when it comes to these non-editing roles.

Consider, too, the demographics element. Many first-time authors pursuing the self-publishing route are retired. They have time and they have resources. They are also experienced in working with "the trades" and will provide coffee and home-made cookies. Caution: as an editor, try not to become a member of the family. This can be difficult, especially as you sit across the table, your hourly-rate clock ticking, and they have begun telling you the story of a recent hospital procedure. You need to find a way to politely raise your pressing editorial question. Smile, say "I wonder if we might ... ," and ask it anyway.

If that doesn't work, try setting in advance an alarm on your cellphone that sounds like an incoming call, timed to interrupt after 20 minutes.

Sometimes editors arrive too late. Your client will have already signed a contract, which you will need to see. Always a delicate request. You will have to help them to decode the basic language of editing and publishing, and you will point out the specifics of their signed agreement. It is no less delicate if the client has a contract but has not yet signed it. In either case, you are providing technical advice about what the contract means to them as an author and what it could mean to you as an editor. Editors do not offer legal advice.

All editors who work with self-publishing authors need to do serious market research here. The list of print/publish providers keeps growing. New companies arrive on the scene, established ones merge, and practices and policies shift. Editors are being inescapably drawn into a consumer-protection role. As an editor, I do not provide legal counsel. That's another professional skill/role that is being bypassed in the culture of self-everything.

13.2.4.2 Working with experienced authors

In the same way that travellers are lucky if they are offered water on some commercial flights these days, the level of author services provided by many commercial publishing houses (unless that author is an international literary celeb) has been seriously curtailed. Contract in hand, experienced authors can be told to find (and pay for) an editor to clean up the work before the publisher sends it on to production. Other experienced authors take a pre-emptive decision: they hire (and pay for) their own editor long before their work arrives at their publisher's offices. Either case opens up an editing niche, although the latter case is a particularly delicate one, because you work for the client, not the publishing house. Don't get caught in the middle. Speak only with your client.

Many experienced authors arrive at the freelance editor's doorstep annoyed that they must now pay for something that was previously part of the service. In this situation, when working directly with the writer, avoid getting drawn into time-consuming conversations about "how it used to be" and try to produce the edit in as little time as possible.

13.2.4.3 Hybrid and indie

The word "indie" in publishing mirrors the shifts that revolutionized the music business two decades ago. Today there's a large and vibrant community of nomadic musicians who travel, often internationally, for months on end, performing live gigs and selling their "merch" at the back of the room. The old model of management by record company has disappeared. Indie musicians do it all themselves: writing, recording, producing, releasing, promoting, and performing on tour. Their web presence, social media, and—increasingly—funding new projects through crowd-sourcing initiatives are all part of the new business model for creators.

Writers are catching up with their musical colleagues. Many choose to bypass the slow gatekeeping processes of established commercial publishers and opt for a hybrid mix of print and online services. Many do it all themselves. The more successful authorpreneurs say they earn more this way compared with the old model of limited royalties offered by mainstream publishers.

These experienced authors can arrive at your digital doorstep with a cavalier kind of confidence that comes with their decision to go indie. Their certainty about the value of their work can be energizing, but also challenging for the editor who is often contracted with reluctance. Each project is an opportunity to explore new possibilities as you learn to edit for multiple platforms, the printed page and the digital screen, all at the same time. Smile as your best suggestions are laughed out of the room.

The entrepreneurial indie spirit of authors can be unsettling for established editors, since it is often accompanied by a grudging "I would do this for myself if I only had the time" conviction. In that case, be sure to manage your time carefully in whatever you do. And, *sotto voce*, since much of this work is built on a different cultural economic model, be prepared to hear about bartering rather than traditional fee structures.

If, like most editors, you have experience in the traditional publishing world as well as in the new world of indie and hybrid publishing, you will need to find a certain serenity about the proliferation of these new kinds of projects that fit comfortably in neither world. Authors, printers, publishers, and web providers are blurring their established roles. And so must we.

13.2.5 Editing trade non-fiction

The phrase "trade non-fiction" describes books and articles that are intended for reasonably well educated general readers. It excludes titles published by academic or genre presses, but includes biographies, memoirs, and subjects ranging from history through ecology and politics to literature, art, and science. The non-fiction titles you find in bookstores fall into this category, as do the articles published in magazines such as *The Walrus*. Readers choose these titles because they want information, analysis, or entertainment—and they expect them to be interesting, well organized, and enjoyable.

The authors who write trade non-fiction are most often experts in their subject areas or journalists, though there are a few professional writers as well. The first two groups in particular often need to work extensively with an experienced editor as they finalize their texts: experts, used to communicating with their peer group, frequently have trouble presenting the content for general readers; and journalists, skilled in writing short columns or essays, may find it difficult to shape the material for a book.

Unfortunately for editors, there are no general guidelines or standards for editing trade non-fiction. Everything depends on the client—schedule, budget, and expectations. Ideally, these manuscripts should be edited at all three levels: a structural edit to organize and present the content in a way that will attract and be accessible for general readers; a stylistic edit to clarify the text and make it a pleasure to read; and a copy edit to make it correct and consistent. To accomplish these tasks, two different editors are sometimes hired, one to do the structural and probably the stylistic work too, and the other to look after the copy editing. Alternatively, one editor with skills in all branches of editing can do the edit, though in two separate passes.

How many clients are willing to hire or to appoint two editors to work on one manuscript? Large trade publishers usually divide the editing between an in-house structural editor (or a trusted outside editor) and a freelance copy editor, with one of them (or perhaps both) responsible for the stylistic edit. All other clients—medium and small trade publishers, institutions and associations, and a rapidly increasing number of self-publishing writers—usually hire only one editor for each project. They don't allow time in the schedule or money in the budget for two editors, and their expectations vary widely from one to another.

13.2.5.1 What is involved in editing trade non-fiction?

There are no style guides for editing trade non-fiction, so the decisions about how much to do are left to the editor. Every manuscript is different, depending on the writer's skill in preparing the text for its intended readers. Let's consider the key elements that editors should evaluate as they decide where to focus their attention.

For further discussion of the editing process, see 13.2.3.

13.2.5.1.1 Structural editing

(a) **Process**: First, read through the entire manuscript quickly, to get a sense of the contents and how the author has organized it. Then pause, think about your instinctive reaction to the text, and make a few notes. Second, make a brief outline of the text in point form. As you look over this summary, do you spot any repetitions, gaps, or breakdowns in parallel structure? By now you should have a good sense of the manuscript's strengths and problems, and you'll be ready to begin your detailed structural edit. In essence you'll be writing a report for the author that clearly sets out your suggestions for major revisions while, at the same time, you annotate the manuscript for particular points. Ideally, the author will revise the text along the lines you suggest, or in some other way after further dialogue, and then return it to you for the stylistic edit. However, if the author is not willing or able to make the revisions, you should be able to implement them yourself. You will then send the revised text to the author for approval.

(b) **Book title**: The title plays a key role in attracting readers to trade non-fiction books or articles. These titles are commonly in two parts: a short, catchy main title, and a longer subtitle that succinctly describes the theme. As the editor, you should check that the title works both to get attention and to pinpoint the content. If your client has sales or publicity staff, you should consult with them as well as with the author before the final title is decided.

(c) **Opening paragraphs**: The opening paragraphs must also grab readers' attention, or readers will put the book or article down, never to return. When you've completed your edit, go back to this all-important section again and assess whether it truly leads into the essence of the text. You may work with your author through several versions before you have the perfect opening.

(d) **The ending**: The ending is equally crucial to success. As they leave the narrative or the argument, readers must feel satisfied in some basic way—a sense of completion, fulfillment, or explanation, or even of paradox or surprise. The story can't suddenly stop but must conclude—carefully, thoughtfully, or brilliantly—and there are myriad possible variations. Again, return to the ending after your detailed edit and cooperate with the author in getting it just right.

(e) **Parts and chapters**: In between the beginning and the end, there are usually several chapters in a book. Each one should advance the narrative or the discussion one notch—and in the right order. As the editor, you'll often suggest changes in the sequencing of chapters—even complete reversals—or you'll merge some chapters and create new divisions. At times you will also consider whether the book's structure would be improved by dividing the text into parts as well as chapters.

Whatever you decide, each unit should be self-contained, with its own opening and conclusion, a fine balance of story, quotations, examples, commentary, and possibly illustrations too, with no "dead spots" to cause readers to lose interest. As the editor, you'll constantly be evaluating whether this scene needs more vivid description to build pictures in readers' minds, that section is boring because of an excess of detail, or another passage is confusing because the author has not included sufficient information for general readers. At times you'll suggest to the writer major or minor cuts; at other times you'll ask for more text.

(f) **Chapter titles**: Chapter titles play a significant role in trade non-fiction books. They too often come in two parts—catchy and descriptive—but they can also be just one phrase. It's best to have them as a matched set, in both style and length, and they should give a clear idea of the content of each chapter. When they are all lined up in the table of contents, they should provide a clear map of the book—the journey from beginning to end.

With the addition of part titles as well as chapter titles, this map depicts the superhighways as well as the highways. As such, the contents page is extremely valuable for readers.

(g) **Graphic elements**: Many non-fiction trade books are text only, but editors should always be questioning whether the addition of pictures, maps, or figures would be useful. All these graphic elements take time to prepare or acquire, so you need to think about this aspect as soon as you become involved in the project. If they are included, you'll have to consider whether they should be grouped together in sections or scattered through the text, and whether the captions should be short or long, telling their own parallel story to the text. The decisions you make will have a significant bearing on the overall tone and mood of the publication.

(h) **Front and end matter**: Editors of trade non-fiction should think about all the options available in the preliminary sections and the end matter of books. If your author is not well known, would it help to have a foreword written by a celebrity in the field? Or should the author write a prologue or a preface to set the scene or explain why he decided to write the book in the first place? At the end of the book, would it be useful to include a select bibliography or perhaps even an appendix to expand on some topic relevant to the theme? If the main text uses endnotes, you'll need a notes section at the back—but if some of the notes are explanatory rather than simply bibliographical and would be useful to readers as they progress through the book, how about splitting the notes between footnotes (at the bottom of the relevant page of text) and endnotes? Almost certainly you'll want an index that includes the names of people and places as well as the themes and subthemes mentioned in the book.

13.2.5.1.2 Stylistic editing

Because trade non-fiction is always discretionary reading—something people choose to do rather than something they have to do—good stylistic editing is often crucial to its success. At this stage, you focus on paragraphs, sentences, and words—and, depending on the author, you will have little or much to do. If she is talented, you may only be suggesting alternatives for often-repeated adjectives; but if she is an expert trying to write for general readers, you may end up rewriting well over half the manuscript. Even journalists need help when they turn to writing books: the short sentences and paragraphs that suit newspaper and magazine columns transfer poorly to the wider book page, so you'll be shaping longer paragraphs and sentences to fit the more generous book format.

All stylistic editors thrive on selecting the perfect word for the meaning and mood their authors want to convey. You'll surround yourself with your favourite thesaurus and usage books and, in the process, condense every manuscript you edit by a minimum of 10 percent. You'll delete all unnecessary words, rid the text of clichés and hackneyed phrases, and keep a vigilant eye for biased phrases that could cause offence. Before you respond automatically to what the style books call a "prejudiced" word, however, consider what the author is trying to do by using it in a particular context. In trade non-fiction, as in fiction, good writers strive for colour, characterization, and other creative effects that require sensitive responses from editors. As ever, use your judgment—and discuss rather than dictate.

13.2.5.1.3 Copy editing

Of the three branches of editing, copy editing is the most common—almost every published text gets a copy edit. It is also the most prescriptive. Like all copy editors, you'll have a style book, which clearly sets out rules or alternatives for correctness (grammar, punctuation, spelling, usage) and consistency (capitalization, treatment of numbers and type, abbreviations, lists, and spelling again). The most popular guide in North America is the venerable *Chicago Manual of Style*, which allows editors to use their best judgment for a particular text in many areas of consistency. This flexibility is particularly important in trade non-fiction (as in fiction) because you are working on a literary text and must be aware of the overall tone as you make your decisions and meet the needs of potential readers.

Many trade publishers have their own house style guides to be used alongside *Chicago*. These short documents dictate on issues such as the serial comma, when to use words or figures for numbers, and spelling choices—including Canadian or American spelling. In the self-publishing market you may well encounter some clients who have preferences you consider eccentric or even wrong, and you'll have to negotiate your way around them.

Some clients include fact checking among your duties, while others make the author responsible for that task. The wise copy editor, however, is always on the lookout for internal inconsistencies of fact within the text and for errors that run counter to her own general knowledge. See 12.3 for more information about fact checking.

13.2.5.2 *Trade non-fiction editors*

The ideal editors for trade non-fiction are multi-talented: they are sensitive to the writers and readers for these publications, aware of the market, and possess superb editing skills in terms of judgment, organization, and language. As one of these editors, you'll be expected to edit titles in a wide range of subjects and know how to make them successful. Because these books are discretionary reading, their success is counted in the number of copies sold. If you can build up a record as the editor of bestsellers and even literary prizewinners, your own reputation will be assured.

What editorial skills do you need to reach this goal? If you work for one of the large trade book publishing companies in Canada, you can specialize either in structural/stylistic editing or in copy editing. But the vast majority of trade non-fiction books (and magazines) are edited by just one person. If you can do only structural editing, for instance, or only copy editing, you will, potentially, tackle only part of the job—if the latter, you will resemble a doctor who can diagnose and treat only common ailments, without any thought of further investigation or referrals to specialists. In this scenario, if the manuscript has severe structural flaws as well as basic language problems, it will receive a meticulous copy edit while the flaws remain.

In the current world of trade non-fiction publishing in Canada, it seems that the editors who are at least competent in all branches of editing will be the most in demand—both by publishers and, as self-publishing writers become more knowledgeable about the process, by these clients too. If you're one of the many editors who feel you are very good in one of these areas but not in the others, you'd be wise to learn enough to be able at least to analyze the problems in any given manuscript and report your findings to your client. Ideally, you should also form a partnership or an understanding with another editor whose skills complement your own so, together, you can complete a full edit for clients who opt for this service. Your work will reflect well on you as a team and on the profession of editing. (For a discussion of manuscript analysis, see 13.2.3.1.)

There's no doubt that writers—particularly trade non-fiction writers who depend on the quality and success of their publications—respect good editing. They want more, not less, of it—and they bond with their editors in the same way that patients bond with their doctors. They know that, together with their editors, they produce great books.

For further reading

Shipton, Rosemary. "The Mysterious Relationship: Authors and Their Editors." In *Editors, Scholars, and the Social Text*, edited by Darcy Cullen, 44–66. Toronto: University of Toronto Press, 2012.

———. "Twelve-Step Editing." *The Editors' Weekly.* http://blog .editors.ca/2014/11/twelve-step-editing.

13.2.6 Editing children's and young adult fiction

The success of all fiction, whether it's intended for young readers or adults, depends on the author's mastery of the building blocks of writerly craft: plot, character, setting, dialogue, point of view, and more. If you're editing books for young readers, you'll need to understand, along with these standard building blocks, other, more specific considerations.

13.2.6.1 Age categories

A paramount consideration is the age of the intended reader. Familiarize yourself with what readers at the target age are looking for. For some editors—this one included—the childhood and teen years have faded unceremoniously into the mists of the distant past, perhaps the Jurassic period. When you feel this alarming sense of disconnection from your more youthful self, putting yourself in the shoes of young readers and understanding what they love or reject in fiction can feel like an insurmountable task. So how can you gain the confidence to edit this material?

Start by getting a grounding in the characteristics of the standard categories of fiction for young readers. This will allow you to determine whether your author is working more or less within established parameters or is somewhere out in left field, writing, for example, a 20,000-word tome for five-year-olds. The particulars of each category can vary according to which research you consult and individual publishers, and there's overlap when it comes to age. View the information that follows as rough guidelines rather than hard-and-fast definitions of each category.

Baby and toddler books (up to age 3): These very short books are rarely longer than about 300 words. Stories, if any, are extremely simple and revolve around common events in a child's life. Often the books consist of rhymes, songs, the alphabet, or numbers. Illustrations naturally dominate, and sometimes fun novelty features like pop-ups, textures, or sounds are included.

Picture books (ages 4 to 8): These rarely exceed about 1,500 words. Plots are extremely basic and typically follow one character's actions. As the name indicates, illustrations are a key component and tell the stories as much as the accompanying text does; they're usually in colour and featured on every page.

Easy readers (ages 6 to 8): This category is intended for kids who are just starting to read on their own. Word count tops out at about 2,000 words. Easy-to-follow single storylines are told mostly through action and dialogue using simple sentences. Very few sentences are used per page, rarely more than half a dozen. The story may be structured into very short chapters for slightly more advanced readers in this group. Like picture books, easy readers tend to be illustrated on each page and usually in colour.

Chapter books (ages 6 to 10): At the bottom end of the age range are books that help young readers make the transition from easy readers to this category. Chapter books are a maximum of about 15,000 words. As you'd expect, slightly more intricate plots and longer, more complex sentences characterize these books. Because readers' attention spans are still short, material is organized into short chapters up to about four pages in length that may end with cliffhangers to encourage readers to continue. These books rely less on illustrations to tell the story than books in the previous categories; artwork is often black-and-white and occurs every few pages.

Middle grade (ages 8 to 12): These books reflect the advanced language skills of their readers. They approach novel length, topping out at about 40,000 words. Plots take more twists and turns than in previous categories and include subplots with secondary characters. Protagonists are typically no more than about 12 years of age and have a character arc, so they undergo growth and change. Because children at this age are inwardly focused, the protagonist is as well, and books deal with themes of interest to kids in this age group—friendship, peers, siblings, school, changing roles and responsibilities, and puberty. Trilogies or lengthy series with a regular cast of characters are popular in middle grade fiction.

Young adult (ages 12 and up): These rich, intricate novel-length works include subplots and a sizable cast of main and secondary characters. One protagonist emerges from among the main characters, invariably a teenager and often a bit older than the reader, representing someone the reader often aspires to be. As with middle grade fiction, protagonists undergo transformation, often triggered by events beyond their immediate sphere that they encounter while making the transition into the adult world. Rather than current trends, themes reflect timeless and universal teenage struggles: finding an identity and a place in the world, understanding one's impact on the world and the consequences of one's actions, developing self-confidence, and handling peer pressure. Many young adult novels are tightly plotted and written, rivalling the best adult fiction in sophistication, so it's not surprising they have crossover appeal to the adult market.

Whatever the target audience, all fiction needs a strong plot that includes an initial conflict, heightening tension, a climax, and a resolution. It also requires believable, engaging, three-dimensional characters. All of this needs to be supported by a rich, fully realized setting. You'll need to help ensure these qualities are in place. As always, the age of your author's readers needs to be considered while editing.

13.2.6.2 Simplifying language

Clear, easy-to-understand language is of paramount importance when editing picture books, easy readers, and chapter books, as readers at these levels are still learning to read.

Very young readers need short, simple sentences, usually in subject-verb-object sequence. Other grammatical structures may confuse them. One idea per sentence works best; it's too much to throw several ideas into one long, complex sentence.

As you would when editing material for adults, eliminate passive voice where possible. If a word seems much too advanced, suggest alternatives to the author or suggest they explain to the reader what the difficult word means (if you think this would work in the context). As well, unless you're sure children would understand them, eliminate figures of speech and idioms, even ones that are very familiar to you. Alternatively, you might suggest that the author explain them if doing so would be appropriate.

How can you be sure that the language used is appropriate for young readers? A number of online readability tools are helpful, such as Readability-Score.com. This site analyzes whatever portion of text you paste in and computes scores on several readability indexes to give you an average grade level. Try several portions of text from the manuscript and average them, as results can vary widely across the text; inevitably, dialogue-heavy passages will rate as a lower grade level than denser, more descriptive ones.

Of course, it's possible to go too far in simplifying text for younger readers, resulting in monotonous prose that children will reject. Books should stimulate and challenge young readers' imaginations, so no matter how simple and clear the prose is, it also needs to be varied and lively. Never be afraid to suggest to an author that she use playful language and nonsense words to engage readers if this would fit the mood of the story. And remember that it's okay if some words are just a little beyond readers. Reading should encourage intellectual growth in a gentle, not overwhelming way, and if kids do have to reach for the dictionary now and then, that's hardly the worst thing that could happen to them.

Difficulty of vocabulary is much less of an issue in middle grade and young adult fiction, since kids reading such books typically have advanced reading skills. In this category, editing becomes more about preventing authors from making a number of common blunders born of misunderstanding the audience. It's clichéd to say that someone should embrace his or her "inner child," but doing so is exactly what it takes to write a convincing book for kids. Editors who work on this sort of material also need to access their younger selves. Young writers and editors may have an edge over mature ones, but we can all learn to edit this material. Let's take a closer look at some of the issues around middle grade and young adult fiction.

13.2.6.2.1 Pacing

Fast pacing and intensity are vital so readers don't drop by the wayside. We live in an impatient era in which multi-tasking and short attention spans are all too common, and kids (not to mention many adults) typically don't have the patience to wait for stories to develop in a leisurely fashion. They're game to take a thrilling ride. Books need to mirror the intensity of their own lives or they'll lose interest. Young adult books in particular are often written in the present tense to underscore both intensity and speed. As well, many of these books feature first-person narrators who contribute immediacy and intimacy, adding a focused and urgent quality. Encourage authors to play up emotion. Pare away wordiness, and to keep the story moving, suggest ditching non-essential backstory or digressions.

13.2.6.2.2 Authenticity in voice

Authenticity is absolutely essential. Take narrative voice, for example. Does the child or teen narrator indeed sound like a kid? Perhaps she's stiff and formal in her speech, sounding like an old fogey and using words that people of her generation just don't. This might fit if the character is a quirky, nerdy outcast, but if she's an "average" kid it's all wrong. Other characters may not seem convincingly young because of their dialogue. Young people often censor themselves less than adults, blurting things out easily. They also use casual, ungrammatical language and hyperbole. Authors shouldn't put a stranglehold on characters who would naturally speak in this fashion, so encourage a looser, more relaxed approach to speech.

Of course, there are limits to exaggerated dialogue. If a character is grating on your nerves, he'll likely annoy readers too, so tone him down. And feel free to excise interrobangs (an exclamation mark and question mark combined), multiple exclamation marks and question marks, superfluous italics, all caps, and bold, which many a youthful writer uses to excess.

Many writers think using slang is the best way to authentically convey contemporary speech. Slang is a convenient shortcut, but it's all too easy to get wrong. Authors may mistakenly use words that were popular in their day—or even last year—but are now obsolete, which confuses and loses readers. "Slang du jour" gets old almost overnight, making a book appear dated very quickly. Encourage authors to use slang sparingly, if at all.

13.2.6.2.3 Authenticity in behaviour

Authenticity also needs to be present in how characters behave. Childhood and adolescence is marked by self-absorption, feelings of uncertainty about fitting in and finding one's way, extremes of feeling, and often impulsive or reckless behaviour that may have damaging consequences. Many kids also have a keen sense of justice and rebel against what they think just isn't right. The best fiction for children and teens heightens these qualities in characters, and if the characters don't react as real teens would in a given situation, readers won't relate to them. Flag any actions that don't ring true and suggest alternatives.

13.2.6.2.4 Authenticity in setting

An authentic setting is essential. Perhaps an author is ostensibly writing about contemporary kids but is actually depicting a familiar setting from her youth 30 years ago. This just won't fly with current young readers. Today's kids live in an often bewilderingly complex society dominated by the influence of technology and social media. Diversity is a fact of life, for classrooms and neighbourhoods are filled with people of every race, cultural background, and sexual orientation and with those with disabilities. Any novel with a contemporary setting needs to reflect the reality kids see around them daily. At the same time, beware of hypersensitivity (see ECE3, 2.1.6).

13.2.6.2.5 Attitude and tone

Eliminate a patronizing or preachy attitude. No one likes to be talked down to, including kids. Dissuade your authors from disrespecting the intelligence of their readers. As well, discourage them from sugar-coating unpleasant truths or insisting on happy endings that are inappropriate to their books. Kids who are reading middle grade and young adult fiction are savvy enough to know that life isn't all unicorns and rainbows, and many of these readers enjoy exploring the shadow side of both themselves and the world around them through fiction. Inherently dark genres, such as paranormal, mystery, and dystopian science fiction, are magnetically attractive to many teens. But although these stories are intentionally grim, it's important for authors to offer a small measure of light in the darkness, for life isn't about unrelenting pessimism. And while stories certainly may contain a message for young readers, encourage authors to deliver it in a subtle, not heavy-handed way so kids don't feel as if they're being hammered with a sermon.

13.2.6.3 Assessing your edit

If you feel disconnected from the kid within you, it's easy to be unsure whether you're getting it right when editing children's and young adult fiction. So beyond readability indexes, how can you gauge whether your edits are on the mark?

A little informal consultation with the experts—kids—is often all that's needed. If you have children or can manage to borrow a few willing ones, run by them any text you're questioning and watch how they respond. Do they understand the writing easily, or are certain words or expressions beyond them? And what do they think of how certain characters in the book speak or react to situations? Young people can quickly ferret out the inauthentic and whatever else isn't working for them.

Social media is also a real boon for gauging whether you're heading in the right direction with your edits. Connect with other editors on Facebook and LinkedIn, and you'll soon have at your disposal the collective wisdom of hundreds, even thousands of editors across the globe. There's bound to be someone who can answer questions like "Do 13-year-olds use the word *dude*?" because they have a teen at home to consult or have just finished editing a series of contemporary young adult novels. Answers are readily available, so helping authors create the best children's and young adult fiction needn't be daunting at all.

For further reading

Backes, Laura. "The Difference Between Middle Grade and Young Adult." Children's Fiction Factor. Accessed October 6, 2014. http://children.fictionfactor.com/articles/differences.html.

———. "Understanding Children's Writing Genres." Children's Fiction Factor. Accessed October 6, 2014. http://children.fictionfactor.com/articles/kidsgenres.html.

Feeney, Nolan. "The 8 Habits of Highly Successful Young-Adult Fiction Authors." The Atlantic [online], October 22, 2013. theatlantic.com/entertainment/archive/2013/10/the-8-habits-of-highly-successful-young-adult-fiction-authors/280722.

Newbery, Linda, and Meg Rosoff. "Genre in Children's Writing." The Guardian [online], September 25, 2008. theguardian.com/books/2008/sep/26/booksforchildrenandteenagers1.

Walker, Jane. "Top Tips for Editing Children's Books." The Publishing Training Centre [blog]. July 18, 2012. train4publishing.co.uk/component/zoo/item/top-tips-for-editing-children-s-books.

13.3 Corporations, not-for-profits, associations, and government

13.3.1 Editing for corporations, not-for-profits, and associations

Corporations, not-for-profit (NFP) organizations, and associations all prepare myriad documents in many formats and media. And many of them hire in-house or freelance editors.

13.3.1.1 Finding clients

Finding clients for these sectors will require looking in different places. Many large corporations advertise in newspapers or use online media. Some place ads on the Editors Canada national job board, some rely on word of mouth, and yet others use a service such as MERX or Charity Village.

MERX (merx.com) lists tenders for private corporations and international markets, as well as governments.

Charity Village (charityvillage.com) is the non-profit sector's largest online recruiting resource. The website allows for searches according to skills and postal code. The listings are free to access. A subscription service supports alerts, saved search results, and a savings on e-learning through the site.

13.3.1.2 Special editing considerations

A corporation, NFP, or association that does business internationally may require communication to be in American or British English. Editors should always know the audience and the market before beginning an edit.

13.3.1.3 Style guides

Corporate, NFP, and association style guides tend to be available for internal use only. Some organizations do not have style guides, a situation that provides an opportunity for an enterprising editor.

13.3.1.4 Standards for communication

Although standards for communication vary depending on the type of organization, most corporations, NFPs, and associations stress the use of plain language to communicate internally and with the public. Communication needs to be clear, concise, coherent, correct, and consistent. This is particularly true when communicating with stakeholders who have lower literacy levels or when communicating with busy executives who have little time to decipher messages.

Information about plain language communication is available at PLAIN, the Plain Language Association International (plain languagenetwork.org). See also ECE3, 2.6.

13.3.2 Editing for government

Governments produce an astonishing array of documents and communication materials each year in a variety of media. The public sector offers a wide range of work for editors with different expertise. It may well be worth the time to pursue opportunities with departments whose work interests you.

Canada has three levels of government: federal, provincial/ territorial, and municipal. Each one has different responsibilities, structures, programs, and policies.

13.3.2.1 Federal

Federal responsibilities generally include those that affect Canadians as a whole, such as foreign policy and international trade, food safety, defence, postal services, money and banking, immigration, pan-Canadian transportation, copyright and patents, criminal law, and economic development.

The federal government's structure comprises smaller operating units:

- Ministries are organizational units of responsibilities. A cabinet minister leads each ministry, which may be made up of one or more departments, agencies, and entities.

- Departments are units within ministries that implement the laws of Parliament, oversee policies, and deliver programs to the public. A cabinet minister leads each department, while a deputy minister administers the department under the guidance of the minister. Departments vary considerably in size.

- Agencies have similar responsibilities to those of departments with respect to legislation, policies, and programs, but they are subject to different administrative rules. Examples include the Canada Border Services Agency, the Public Health Agency of Canada, and the Canadian Environmental Assessment Agency.

- Crown corporations operate under acts of Parliament as separate entities. Examples include the Canada School of Public Service, Canada Post Corporation, and VIA Rail Canada Inc.

- Tribunals, boards, councils, and commissions all serve specific purposes; they make decisions or recommendations, review issues, or oversee specific infrastructure or sites.

For an up-to-date list of Government of Canada departments, agencies, and entities, visit canada.ca/en/gov/dept. Most departments and units produce annual reports, audit reports, and accountability reports to Parliament; maintain a website and social media accounts; and communicate with the public. All provide opportunities for editors.

13.3.2.2   Provincial and territorial

Provincial and territorial responsibilities include health care, education, welfare, the administration of justice, and transportation within their boundaries. Two of the territories—Yukon and the Northwest Territories—are increasingly assuming province-like responsibilities such as joint control over natural resources with the federal government. Contact the individual province or territory for current lists of departments and agencies. Most produce many reports, providing opportunities for editors.

13.3.2.3   Municipal

Municipal governments—a few of which are larger than some provincial governments—are responsible for water, sewer, and waste management; parks and recreation; libraries and community centres; animal control; local economic development; planning, zoning, and building permits; fire prevention and policing; and public transportation. There are approximately 4,000 municipal governments across the country, providing many opportunities for editors both in-house and freelance.

13.3.2.4   *Indigenous affairs*

Indigenous affairs has traditionally been the responsibility of the federal government. Increasingly, though, Indigenous communities are assuming responsibility for governing their own land and function in a manner similar to that of municipal councils. Most produce a number of reports and maintain a website, and therefore work with editors.

13.3.2.5   *Kinds of federal government documents*

Although the following list is not exhaustive, it provides a glimpse into the vast array of documents the federal government produces. Provincial, territorial, municipal, and Indigenous governments will also produce many kinds of reports.

Control documents communicate corporate philosophy and implement mission and vision statements. They ensure consistency, help to maintain quality control, and improve efficiency and productivity. They may include the following documents:

- Mission and vision statements.

- Constitution.

- Bylaws.

- Codes of conduct.

- Legislation.

- Regulations. According to the Cabinet Directive on Regulatory Management, "Regulation is a key policy instrument used by government to enable economic activity and to protect the health, safety, security, and environment of Canadians." Regulations have a life cycle that allows for systematic evaluation and review, including of time-based performance indicators.

- Policies and procedures. These are preventative documents. Policies set out directions for realizing the organization's mission and implementing its vision statement. Procedures, on the other hand, comprise a set of instructions in support of a policy.

- Directives and standards. These provide mandatory operational or technical measures or practices. Guidelines provide operational direction or further explanation.

Statutory documents: Many compliance documents follow from regulation. These include annual *Reports on Plans and Priorities* (RPPs) and *Departmental Performance Reports* (DPRs), both of which require the services of in-house or freelance editors. The Auditor General's audit reports fall into this category.

Reports to and communication with the public: These include annual reports (which usually include audit reports), websites, communiqués, and social media communications.

13.3.2.6   *Finding government clients*

No matter how small your business, you can sell your services directly to governments. Here are tips for landing Government of Canada contracts.

- **Take free seminars and webinars across Canada on selling to the federal government.** Check the Event Calendar at buyandsell.gc.ca (buyandsell.gc.ca/event-calendar), a procurement portal for suppliers and federal buyers. Or ask staff to email you a link to a pre-recorded webinar.

- **Register in the Supplier Registration Information database at buyandsell.gc.ca.** This will give you your Procurement Business Number—mandatory to get paid by Public Works and Government Services Canada (the main shopping arm of government) and other departments.

- **Employ short-, medium-, and long-term sales tactics to improve your chances.** The more ways a federal client can purchase your services, the better. See the following tips for ideas.

  - **Subcontract (short-term).** Work for a company or temporary help services agency that already has a contract. Find candidates at buyandsell.gc.ca by searching "Awards," "Standing Offers and Supply Arrangements," or the "Contract History" database (all found under

"Procurement Data"). You can also check Treasury Board's "Proactive Disclosure" section for all departments (tbs-sct. gc.ca/pd-dp/index-eng.asp).

- **Get on source lists and government-wide procurement tools (medium-term).** Departmental source lists are for contracts up to $25,000. Approach departments and agencies that match your expertise. Email other managers relevant to your sector, too (check the Government Electronic Directory Services, known as GEDS; geds.gc.ca/en/ GEDS?pgid=002). Also, apply to get on government-wide procurement tools like ProServices, a mandatory tool for many professional sevices contracts up to $80,400 (tpsgc-pwgsc.gc.ca/app-acq/sp-ps/index-eng.html). See a full list of procurement tools at buyandsell.gc.ca /goods-and-services.

- **Bid on tenders (long-term).** Tenders for larger contracts are posted on buyandsell.gc.ca. Proposals are time-consuming but can pay off, especially if you win a standing offer or supply arrangement award. Standing offers are offers from a potential supplier to provide services at pre-arranged prices, under set terms and conditions, when required. They are not a guarantee of work. However, they are often the first step in landing regular work from the government. If the department calls up someone from the list of those who are on a standing offer, work will follow. These lists of pre-qualified suppliers last three to four years or longer.

• **Market yourself constantly.** Let materiel managers and others know if you've been awarded a standing offer or supply arrangement. From time to time, email the service manager who needs the work completed or the contract authority on your standing offer or supply arrangement to let them know if you're available and have acquired any helpful new skills.

• **Do your research.** Read reports from departments you're targeting (such as annual reports on plans and priorities). Stay abreast of Treasury Board policies key to your field (tbs-sct. gc.ca/pol/index-eng.aspx). Check buyandsell.gc.ca for news. Peruse the Throne Speech, and scour the online magazine Canadian Government Executive (canadiangovernment executive.ca).

- **Know the Government of Canada fiscal planning cycle.** The first quarter (April to June) is for setting budgets. The second quarter (July to September) is for establishing programs and work plans. The third quarter (October to December) is for purchasing. And the very busy fourth quarter (January to March) is for wrapping everything up. This means that there tends to be more freelance work in the final months of the fiscal year.

- **Contact other governments, too.** Visit marcan.net for leads on contracting to Canadian provincial and territorial governments. Canada also has trade agreements with other countries (such as the United States; see sell2usgov.ca) that include government procurement. More markets to conquer! Check individual provincial and municipal websites for more information about their procurement processes.

13.3.2.7 Plain language editing

Specific training in plain language writing and editing is an asset for editors who want to find work in the government sector. (For a discussion of plain language, see ECE3, 2.6.)

The Government of Canada and many provincial and municipal governments stipulate that communication with the public should be in plain language. The Communication Policy of the Government of Canada states that Canadian institutions have a duty to inform the public and that this "includes the obligation to communicate effectively. Information about policies, programs, services and initiatives must be clear, relevant, objective, easy to understand and useful."

The policy also states that this requirement applies to internal communication and reports to Parliament, both written and oral.

13.3.2.8   Government style guides

The Canadian Style is the official style guide of the Government of Canada. It is available free of charge online at Termium (click on "Writing Tools" at btb.termiumplus.gc.ca). The print version was last updated in 1997, but some sections of the electronic version have been updated. The Translation Bureau, which is responsible for Termium and the Language Portal of Canada, will continue to update *The Canadian Style* as required.

Despite there being an overarching Government of Canada style, many departments and even some divisions have their own style guides. Many (such as the new Canada.ca Web Content Style Guide for the new Canada.ca website for all government departments) are available only internally.

A few of the publicly available guides are listed below:

- Industry Canada has some of the best online resources available to all. *Industry Canada Style Guide for Writers and Editors* is a detailed style guide that covers many of the questions editors have about government documents, including capitalization, titles, and reference notes. Industry Canada also has a site for Industry Canada Corporate Identity and FIP Standards (FIP is the Federal Identity Program), various layout templates, and editing and proofreading checklists. (All can be found by searching "publishing toolbox" at ic.gc.ca.)

- The Canadian Institutes of Health Research (CIHR) has a style guide that details how to reference CIHR and its partners, hyphenate words and expressions that are commonly used at CIHR, and punctuate and capitalize text (cihr-irsc .gc.ca/e/44167.html).

It is always a good idea to check with clients for their specific style guides and preferences before beginning any edit.

13.3.2.9   Government standards for communication

All official Government of Canada communication with the public must be available in French and English, written in plain language, display a clear and consistent corporate identity, be accessible, reflect the diversity of Canadian society, and communicate risk, where applicable.

This means that often, documents or official communications are written in English or French, edited in the language of their writing, and then translated into the other official language. Ideally, translations should be edited, including a concordance or comparative edit to proof and verify the translated version. This process is described in an article available on the Language Portal: "Comparative Revision: An Essential Step" (noslangues-ourlanguages.gc.ca/en/blogue-blog/revision-comparative-eng).

While the Translation Bureau is the Government of Canada's centre of expertise in translation services, departments can and do use other translation service providers.

Translators are skilled language professionals with the specific expertise, cultural knowledge, and specialized resources required to convey a message accurately in a second language. In Canada, certified translators belong to provincial associations that regulate the profession. A national organization, the Canadian Translators, Terminologists and Interpreters Council, is made up of eight provincial and territorial organizations. Many translators, however, do not receive specific training in editing as part of their education, nor are they tested for it. For this reason, translated documents should be edited.

Editors who work for the federal government do not necessarily have to be bilingual, but it can help to have a working knowledge of French when editing in English. The government hires many English editors on a freelance basis each year; editors with some knowledge of French can provide added value by recognizing where errors lurk in translated documents and flagging text that may require clarification or changes.

13.3.2.10 Government resources for editing

The best resource for government editing is the Language Portal of Canada (noslangues-ourlanguages.gc.ca/index-eng.php). It contains a number of links that provide valuable resources to editors and language buffs alike. They can all be accessed through the Language Portal or on their own. All are available free of charge to the public.

- Termium Plus is the Government of Canada's official terminology and linguistic database. It provides translations for almost four million English and French terms as well as 200,000 Spanish terms. It can be personalized in "My Termium," which will save a list of frequently used terms.

- Peck's English Pointers. Written by editor Frances Peck, these interactive quizzes provide a self-test for common errors and misconceptions.

- HyperGrammar2 was adapted from an online tutorial developed by the Department of English at the University of Ottawa. This self-teaching tool is designed to help improve one's knowledge of English grammar.

- The Canadian Style, the official style guide for the Government of Canada, is described at 13.3.2.8.

- Word Tailoring is a dictionary-like reference tool for finding English equivalents for French words or phrases.

- Favourite Articles is a collection of articles from the Translation Bureau's periodical, Language Update. It provides information on the latest decisions about usage, style, and language-related problems.

- The Our Languages blog contains articles written by external contributors, including Editors Canada.

The site also contains quizzes and links to resources such as Glossaries and Dictionaries, Indigenous Languages, Writing Resources, Language Learning, and Organizations and Events.

The Language Portal also has an ourlanguages.gc.ca on the go! app for searching French and English terms on smart phones and tablets.

13.3.2.11 *Special considerations*

Editors working on government documents should be prepared to obtain security clearance. You can increase your chances of finding work by offering value-added services such as production management, understanding the need to combine different kinds of editing in "an edit," and investing time in getting to know how governments work and who hires editors.

13.3.2.11.1 Security clearance

Editing government documents often requires reliability status or security clearance for everyone who has access to the document. There are five levels:

- Basic reliability status is for non-sensitive information.

- Enhanced reliability status is required when the contractor or employee has access to designated (protected) information and assets.

- Level I security clearance is required when the contractor or employee has access to confidential information and documents.

- Level II security clearance is required when the contractor or employee has access to secret information and documents.

- Level III security clearance is required when the contractor or employee has access to top-secret information and documents.

The process to get a security clearance certificate may take some time. If you have been awarded a standing offer, the federal buyer will sponsor you to get security clearance if you have asked to be sponsored, regardless of whether you get a call-up for work. Individuals and firms can go through Public Works and Government Services Canada (PWGSC) to obtain their own security clearance, but this takes much longer, as PWGSC gives precedence to those named in pending contracts. For more information, see PWGSC's Industrial Security Program (tpsgc-pwgsc. gc.ca/esc-src/index-eng.html).

Major security clearance changes are in the works as a result of a Treasury Board policy change in late 2014. Now everyone—even independent contractors—needs to have an organizational clearance as well as a personal clearance. More info is available here: theproposalcentre.ca/wp-blog/2014/08/08/ ind-contractors-registration.

13.3.2.11.2 Scheduling and production management

Whether working in-house (e.g., temporary position) or on contract, editors may also be asked to perform production management duties, such as assigning editorial jobs, reviewing the quality of editorial work, or overseeing the schedules and work of writers, editors, translators, and designers. A thorough knowledge of the production process is an asset when working on larger documents or documents that will be disseminated in a variety of media.

For a discussion of production considerations, see 13.2.1.

13.3.2.11.3 Types of edits

Although Editors Canada recognizes four distinct types of editing and certifies editors in them (see 12.2), many editors working for the federal government are required to perform "an edit" that may comprise parts of a structural edit, a stylistic edit, a copy edit, and a proofread. If this is the case, build in sufficient time for a number of passes during the editing process.

For more on editing in passes, see 13.2.3.2.1.

13.3.2.11.4 Government employees who hire editors

Communications managers and other managers who are responsible for producing documents and publications often require the services of an editor to help produce publications, particularly if they are not familiar with the publishing process. You have an excellent opportunity to market yourself as an expert who understands the milieu and can offer a solution. For many departments, you can use the Departmental Listing on GEDS to find Communications staff (sage-geds.tpsgc-pwgsc.gc.ca). Jobs are listed on jobs.gc.ca.

13.4 Educational materials

13.4.1 Market overview

A handful of large publishing houses dominate the educational market in Canada. With ongoing acquisitions, mergers, and relocations outside the country, there were barely three big publishers left at the time of writing. The kindergarten to grade 12 market (K–12) has been particularly hard hit, some say because of changes to copyright laws that make extensive photocopying for educational purposes less of an infringement.

Small publishers often dip into the educational market with individual titles. A growing number of independent publishers offer some specialized approach or product, often catering to a single subject or product line. Packagers are another source of editing work, as publishers outsource projects to these one-stop shops.

"Product" is an important notion. The educational market is not publishing textbooks alone. Workbooks, teacher guides, software, animations and videos, ready-made interactive whiteboard lessons, test banks, and websites are just some of the suite of products in a "program" produced for classroom use.

Outside of the publishing realm, corporations are producing classroom materials to either entice class visits (field trips) or to promote their message (conservation being a typical one). They appeal to teachers' needs to engage students with lively and relevant content that meets learning expectations, and so they get their message into the classroom.

There is a great deal of work available for freelancers in the educational market, especially for those editors with extra credentials in teaching or in a subject area. Freelancers may be used at almost any stage of the publishing process, from structural/developmental editing through to permissions and picture research.

13.4.1.1 Authors and editors

Publishers conceive of a large portion of products in the K–12 market, and their choices are market-driven, often born of revised curriculum guidelines from the ministries of education. In the higher-education market, front-line instructors have an idea that they turn into a book. But in school divisions, the publishers have the ideas and hire respected expert teachers (and often a team of them) to write the books.

In the case of the publisher-driven project, authors have far less authority than in mass-market publishing. Authors are often novice writers, too. The editor—with so many criteria to meet, with a novice writer who is typically maintaining a full-time teaching schedule, and with a publishing timeline that is tight and tied to critical dates in the school calendar—often wields a very heavy hand and often drafts materials for the author or slathers on stylistic changes to make team-written material sound cohesive and satisfy the product profile. The structural editor (called the developmental editor in this niche) is called upon to assess the strengths of the writer and to compensate in any way necessary, diplomatically. Project managers therefore look for developmental editors who are good writers.

13.4.1.2 *Stakeholder and peer review*

Having a manuscript reviewed by a slew of peers and subject experts is typical. Indigenous Elders may be invited to advise on accurate, appropriate, and adequate representations of their world views related to the subject matter. Besides the obvious value of having reviewers fact check and flag concerns of any kind (often called the technical check), this stage gets the manuscript into the hands of influential people in the market and makes them part of the team.

Oftentimes key reviewers are flagged and their feedback is proportionally weighted. Input from ministry of education staff, for example, is heavily weighted.

In the case of materials wherein safety might be an issue (for example, anything involving experiments or classroom activities), a safety reviewer is also sought.

13.4.2 Spelling, punctuation, and other matters of style

Guidelines of provincial ministries of education may restrict the style choices for some books. Books intended for Canadian schools must use SI/metric units of measurement, as must most college and university texts.

For a discussion of Canadianizing educational materials, see ECE3, chapter 1, "Canadianization," in particular 1.2.1–1.2.3.

For a discussion of bias and inclusion in educational materials, see ECE3, 1.4.1.

13.4.3 Corollary knowledge

There is a strong tendency for publishers to seek out educational editors who know particular subject areas. There is also a preference for editors with a teaching background. The most valuable developmental editor will also be able to identify gaps in content or pedagogy and coach the writer through filling them in (or draft materials for them).

Developmental editors must also consider how class time and resources, learning expectations, and learning/teaching theories influence and are influenced by a resource's design, function, and structure. Copy editors and proofreaders should have at least an awareness of these issues so that they understand how suggested changes will affect them.

13.4.3.1 *Learning and teaching theory*

To ensure that materials are written at a level appropriate to the developmental stage of the learner and in line with current theories on learning and teaching, the editor must understand these principles well enough to flag concerns. At the least, the editor's understanding in these areas serves to ensure that these vital considerations are not inadvertently edited out of the work.

These theories include but are not limited to

- cognitive (brain) development
- reading level calculations and adjustment strategies
- progression of knowledge within curriculum over the grades
- Bloom's taxonomy
- learning styles and multiple intelligences
- differentiated instruction
- English language learners (ELL)
- student assessment.

13.4.3.2   *Ministry learning expectations/curriculum documents*

Since many products are designed to suit a specific course, the most valuable editor makes informed edits by first understanding the curriculum expectations put out by the ministry of education (or whichever body is related). In the end, books that best match the learning outcomes have the greatest marketability.

13.4.3.3   *Art manuscripts*

Developing art manuscripts (sketches and sources for maps, photos, and illustrations) is an essential skill for the developmental/structural editor working in the educational market. Along with art samples and descriptions, a tracking spreadsheet (log) is usually prepared, and the developmental editor, production editor, and picture researcher contribute as much as they know. Details such as a general description (e.g., entire tree), specifics (e.g., sugar maple with red leaves), finished size (e.g., 1/8 page vertical), recommended or known source, and status of the permission, final image, and required credit lines are listed on the tracking sheet.

For more on editing visuals, see 13.10.

13.5   Academic materials

13.5.1   Scholarly monographs and books

University presses and researchers publish scholarly monographs and books to spread academic ideas.

- Many academics will write textbooks or handbooks that encapsulate their expertise for the benefit of students or industry.

- Multi-author books bring together research on a theme from many people, and are often guided by a volume editor who is responsible for collecting the chapters and sometimes ensuring certain standards of consistency.

- A scholarly monograph is a book or booklet on a single subject by a single subject matter specialist. These may be expanded theses or dissertations.

Editors may be hired by the author, the university, or the publisher. The style and conventions of a university textbook or industry handbook will be quite different from those of a book-length scholarly work. In fact, some academic publications are now being published exclusively as ebooks, involving a publication process that may affect the work an editor is asked to do.

Academic presses often have publication committees and peer reviewers that offer advice on the quality of a manuscript and whether or not to publish it. An author can enhance a manuscript's chance of being published by hiring an editor before submitting the manuscript to a publishing house.

Before beginning work, clarify the budget, time constraints, and tasks that are reasonable. For example, if a budget is limited, the author might fact check notes and references instead of relying on the editor to do it. To stay within the budget or to maintain author voice, editors may be asked to edit with a light hand.

Likely style guide choices for academic works include field-specific guides, such as the American Psychological Association's *Publication Manual* or the Council of Science Editors' *Scientific Style and Format*, or more generic ones, such as *The Chicago Manual of Style*. Various publishing houses and academic presses have developed in-house style guides for authors and editors to follow.

If the author has not yet secured a publisher, the editor may ask the author for a likely publisher and use that publisher's preferred style guide. Even if the publisher hires its own copy editor, evidence that the manuscript has already been professionally edited may help the paper be accepted.

The author of a monograph is an expert in the field and thus may follow specific conventions or use language with which an editor may not be familiar. Editors who are subject matter experts are usually more alert to inconsistencies and issues with notation and terminology; however, being a subject matter expert is not a prerequisite to being a good academic copy editor for many subjects. What's more important is that you can read critically and think logically and rationally to note errors, inconsistencies, and omissions in the argument.

Scholarly books and monographs use notes extensively and often include substantial documentation. With multi-author books, the editor is responsible for consistency across chapters in spelling, numbers, captions, and other areas, as directed. Editors not experienced with academic works can easily miss important omissions or problems, so greater caution and careful consultation of guidelines and references is important.

Edited manuscripts that were written by multiple authors may be sent back to individual authors for review, or the volume editor may be responsible for accepting revisions. Editors of multi-author works require a greater degree of assurance than those of smaller works, usually gained by experience, expertise, familiarity with the subject matter, and a willingness to query the right people to set styles for the whole.

13.5.2 Journals

Academic journals have rigorous style guides that are usually easily accessed online. Be aware that their treatment of specialized subject matter may differ slightly from the advice found in generalized style guides. Take the time to study these journal style guides. Your client may be able to guide you to the website of the journal to which the manuscript will be submitted. If you cannot find a style guide, look for articles in that journal and carefully study the details.

Part of a journal article editor's job is to know the journal's style requirements and ensure that the manuscript matches the expected format. Journals may return articles to authors if they have submitted something that is too far from the desired format.

Whether or not you know which specific journal an author will be submitting to, be aware of the general styles used for numbers, measurements, and specialized terminology particular to that academic field (e.g., italicization and capitalization of species names or exhibition titles, or the correct way to write scientific notation).

Because of the specialized need to be able to assess the argument in high-level research papers, it is a good idea to be well versed in the subject area. Being a subject matter expert is particularly useful when editing engineering, scientific, and legal papers because there are certain conventions of notation, terminology, and techniques that must be applied correctly. Assess your abilities honestly and be clear with your client if you feel there is a limitation. Plenty of professional editors, however, have continued their learning and become experts in subjects that were not their original specialties.

Any extra reading and training that you need to get yourself up to speed is usually considered your own professional development expense, and not to be charged to the client. You will become familiar with the guidelines typical to the journals your clients prefer. If you do an excellent job for a reasonable rate, the repeat business (and extended business through word of mouth) will pay you back for the reading and training at the outset.

Researchers and academic writers, perhaps more than other authors, can become buried in their subject matter and may forget the needs of the outside reader. Therefore, be on the lookout for logical introduction and flow of the argument in the paper. It's also vital to clarify with the author who the intended audience is. If it's a small, specialized audience, then the author can get away with more jargon. If it's a wider audience, the author may need to be prompted to simplify the language.

Many university-trained writers believe they must use only the passive voice or must never write in the first person. In fact, many journals today allow researchers to speak about their own work in the active voice and in the first person. A worthwhile read for the use of active voice and first person in academic writing is Matthew Stevens's book *Subtleties of Scientific Style*.

The editor may be expected to correct tables, photos, maps, charts, and diagrams, so an ability to read and understand any technical details and know their conventional presentation standards is important. Authors may have valid reasons for creating a new symbol or term, but if you suspect that something is off, especially if you can find examples of something similar in the literature, point them out to the author. The author may be grateful that you found a more common or standard way.

Always err on the side of modesty when suggesting editorial changes to academic papers. Rather than making changes wholesale, query authors first. Looking up unfamiliar terms, formats, and notations may also solve mysteries. Unusual constructions or notations that would never be found in *The Chicago Manual* may be quite common in certain academic fields.

A good editor always queries instead of letting a suspicion that something is unusual go unmentioned. Word your query diplomatically. The language that you use in your comments is often the way you can build trust and rapport with your author. It is worth editing your comments to make sure that you come across as both friendly and confident without being too critical or cranky.

University researchers may have funds for editing in their department budgets, and often will maintain relationships with favourite editors for decades. They will also pass along the names of favourite editors to their colleagues. This is a big market, and it is worth developing these client relationships.

13.5.3 Theses and dissertations

The terms "thesis" and "dissertation" are often used interchangeably. Some institutions may insist on hard-and-fast differences between the two, but other parties will insist just as much in the opposite direction.

Theses and dissertations are different from other scholarly writing because they are specifically used to assess whether a university student will earn a degree. Therefore, it is particularly important that editors of theses and dissertations be aware that this piece of writing is a test, and the degree of "help" given should have limits. The Editors' Association of Canada's Guidelines for Ethical Editing of Theses/Dissertations is available for free at editors.ca/hire/theses.html.

It is a good idea to get the supervisor's permission to work with the student on the thesis or dissertation. A conversation can make it clear what degree of help the supervisor considers fair. As well, if the supervisor is aware that the student is using editing services, they may be able to help with the budget.

The editorial roles and responsibilities described in 13.5.1 and 13.5.2 apply as well to theses and dissertations.

Student writers may be more open than the average client to hearing about why you have made changes, and may appreciate coaching comments. Many professionals do some sort of pro bono work, and editors often choose to give students a lower rate to make editing affordable, in exchange for the pleasure of teaching. But do not undersell yourself too far; you are not obliged to offer a discount. If you do, go into these relationships with your eyes wide open—choose people whom you enjoy working with, so that you do not come to resent your reduced rate or flat-rate fee.

You can coach clients with small budgets to perform some of the editing and checking tasks themselves. To reduce the time you would spend editing a long doctoral or master's thesis, you might suggest that the student send you the first few thousand words to which you would make some changes and add coaching-type comments, and that they then attempt to apply those changes throughout later sections. Be creative, and many situations can be made to work for mutual pleasure and benefit.

13.5.4 International clients for academic editing—a great Canadian opportunity

13.5.4.1 Finding work

Canadian editors often get their international scholarly contracts through word of mouth, Editors Canada's Online Directory of Editors (editors.ca/ode/search), and the international copy editors' email list Copyediting-L (copyediting-l.info). They may also establish long-term editing relationships through volunteering, committee work, or connections made through their own research careers. You might also get to know international colleagues through social media, such as the Editors' Association of Earth Facebook page.

Certain firms that headhunt in Canada offer a clearing-house approach to editing high volumes of papers from Asia and India.

These companies may not pay very much, but they have strict style guides and standards and offer excellent mentorship and training opportunities for editors looking to expand their horizons. They may also offer work-abroad opportunities and fine friendships.

Remember, every single freelance job you do pays in more than money. It pays in training, experience, and long-term relationships. It is for that reason, conversely, that you should reject any contract, regardless of money, that comes with a draining relationship, has the potential to damage your reputation, or otherwise does not feel right. Work primarily on jobs that you love!

For further reading

Lioy, Dan T. *Guidelines for Converting a Thesis or Dissertation into an Academic Book or Monograph. Conspectus* 15 (2013). http://reference.sabinet.co.za/webx/access/electronic_journals/conspec/conspec_v15_a11.pdf.

Stevens, Matthew. *Subtleties of Scientific Style.* 2007. sabotin.ung.si/~sstanic/teaching/CIS/references/Stevens-Subtleties_of_Scientific_Style.pdf.

13.6 Poetry, plays, and screenplays

As an editor, you may be asked to edit poetry, plays, and screenplays. All three present special challenges, and editors undertaking work in these areas need to be familiar with these genres. In the case of plays and screenplays, this means not just watching plays or films but studying them in their printed forms and reading books or attending workshops on the craft of playwriting and screenwriting.

13.6.1 Poetry

One dictionary defines poetry as "writing that formulates a concentrated imaginative awareness of experience in language chosen and arranged to create a specific emotional response through meaning, sound, and rhythm."

As such, it is an extremely subjective genre, and in these days of self-publishing, you may be called upon to edit poetry that ranges from simplistic rhyming couplets to what is

essentially
  prose spaced
out
on a page

to near-impenetrable experiments in language and abstraction.

Following are some things to consider when editing poetry.

13.6.1.1 *The first rule: respect voice*

As with any genre of writing, respect the poet's voice, even if it is an amateur voice or a voice that holds no personal appeal for you.

13.6.1.2 *The big picture*

When assessing the big picture, consider the following:

- If the poet is publishing a chapbook, how does it work on a structural level?

- If the book isn't organized on thematic or chronological lines, does the order of the poems work?

- Does the book start strong and end strong?

- Does the sequence of poems work in terms of rhythm, pacing, and flow?

- Are there any poems that seem weak and could be cut? (Often a poet hangs on to those because they have personal emotional significance; be diplomatic when enquiring about the weak ones.)

- Is the title of the collection evocative and memorable, and does it relate in some way to the poems?

13.6.1.3 *The middle ground*

Looking at each individual poem, and keeping the skill level of the poet in mind, consider the following elements:

- **Structure**: Does the poem have a form or shape? If it doesn't, is that deliberate and can it be justified? If the poem involves a narrative or story, does it move toward some insight, climax, or epiphany? If the poem purports to use a traditional structure (e.g., sonnet, villanelle), is it true to the form?

- **Content**: Does the content involve any "concentrated imaginative awareness of experience"? Does it elicit an emotional response? Are there weak lines or phrases that can be strengthened or trimmed?

- **Lines and line breaks**: Is there some logic to the length of the lines? Are the line breaks effective?

- **Rhythm and metre**: Read the poem aloud. Does it work rhythmically? Does the rhythm suit the subject matter (or deliberately contrast with it)? If the poet is employing regular metre, is it used consistently?

- **Rhyme**: If the poems employ rhyming schemes, do they do so consistently?

- **Diction**: Is the diction appropriate to the subject matter? Does the poet have "crutch" words that recur in many of the poems?

- **Imagery**: Is there any? Is it original, or is it clichéd? The same applies to the poet's use of simile and metaphor.

13.6.1.4   *The details*

The final step is to do a copy edit for grammar, spelling, style issues, and punctuation, keeping in mind that some poets use punctuation sparingly or idiosyncratically. It may not be worth arguing about a comma or dash (or a lack thereof) if it doesn't distract or confuse. Similarly, there is no rule about whether or when the first word of a line should be capped, and there's no need to make all the poems consistent in this matter.

For further reading

Ossmann, April. "Thinking Like an Editor: How to Order Your Poetry Manuscript." Poets & Writers, March/April 2011. pw.org/content/thinking_like_an_editor_how_to_orderyour _poetry_manuscript_0.

Rahim, Sameer. "The Mystery of Poetry Editing: From T.S. Eliot to John Burnside." *The Telegraph*, January 23, 2012. telegraph.co.uk/culture/books/9025194/The-mystery-of-poetry-editing-from-TS-Eliot-to-John-Burnside.html.

13.6.2 Plays and screenplays

As an editor, if you've had no experience in the worlds of film or theatre, you should offer to do no more than a copy edit (shading into a line edit) or proofread. Plays and films each involve specific sets of conventions to be followed—or broken, as the writer sees fit—and you need to be familiar with these before undertaking a structural edit.

For example, most commercial films involve a three-act structure, which corresponds to standard storytelling convention (a beginning, a middle, and an end). But they usually also contain set elements such as the inciting incident, the midpoint twist, and the climax or confrontation. Modern plays, on the other hand, tend to be either one act or two acts. In both film and theatre, each act is also usually internally structured to include a setup, some sort of dramatic conflict, and a climax.

When doing a copy edit, look out as well for obvious problems such as

- chronological or other inconsistencies

- failure of story logic

- characters whose voices all sound the same

- no clear dramatic arc

- wooden dialogue.

Also, pay attention to scenes, in film especially, that don't follow the "get in late, get out early" rule—a rule that is often useful in fiction writing, too. For example, unless it's crucial to the plot or required for suspense, we don't need to see Sophia walk up to a house, knock on the door, and wait for Ivan to let her in, then for Ivan to take her coat and usher her into the living room. We can cut straight to her in the living room saying, "Ivan, I've got some bad news." Similarly, at the end of the scene we don't need to see Sophia saying, "Well, I have to go now. Goodbye," put her coat back on, exit the house, and walk to the street. The scene can probably end on her shaking her head and saying, "I'm sorry," or a shot of Ivan's devastated face.

13.6.2.1 Format

In both plays and screenplays, formatting is important. There is no specific Canadian style for these genres. With plays, the formatting for a published script may vary from that of a working script, and the publisher should provide a style sheet. Working play scripts may look more like film scripts.

13.6.2.2 Plays

The first page is the title page. The second page includes the dramatis personae (cast of characters), often with the names in full caps and followed by a brief description (e.g., "JACQUES, a heavy-set man in his mid-40s"). This page, if there is room, also includes a few lines describing the setting (e.g., "Various locations in Lowertown Ottawa") and the time (e.g., "Late winter, 1950"). Setting and time can also go on a third page if there is no room on the dramatis personae page.

Scenes are numbered, and scene titles appear in full caps, centred. Characters' names always appear in full caps, both before lines of dialogue and in stage directions. With dialogue, the name is followed by a colon. Stage directions appear within parentheses. Note that current practice tends to keep stage directions to a minimum.

If the writer indicates that the formatting for a working script is correct, check that the formatting is consistent. Information on formatting a working play script, and an example, can be found at the Cary Playwrights Forum (caryplaywrightsforum.org/wp-content/uploads/2012/07/CPF_play_formatting2.pdf).

Here is an example of the format that Playwrights Canada Press uses:

Act One, Scene Two

Lights up on MARIA, who stands downstage at the kitchen table.

MARIA   (banging the table) I've had enough of this! I've had enough!

TOM and JACQUES enter running.

JACQUES   What the heck? (to MARIA) What's the matter?

13.6.2.3   Screenplays

Industry standard in North America for formatting film scripts is quite specific. It requires Courier 12-point font, left margins 1.5 inches, right margins 1.0 inches, and so on, with some small variations (e.g., in margin widths) allowed.

A number of software programs exist for screenwriting that automatically format scripts correctly; Final Draft is the program most used in the Hollywood industry. Scripts produced in that program cannot be exported to, for example, Microsoft Word for editing. They can, however, be converted to PDFs, and an editor can use a PDF markup program to make edits (see 12.6.4).

The trend in the past couple of decades has been to a leaner, cleaner style of script, with more white space, less narrative description, and fewer instructions to actors. "Interior" and "Exterior" are abbreviated to "Int." and "Ext." Omit camera directions (e.g., "ZOOM IN," "DISSOLVE TO") except where absolutely essential (e.g., "Phone conversations between JACQUES and TOM are SPLIT-SCREEN"). These will get added if the film goes into production and the script becomes a shooting script.

The play sample in 13.6.2.2 would look something like this if converted to a film script:

```
Int. LOWERTOWN OTTAWA APARTMENT KITCHEN

          DAY
MARIA repeatedly bangs the kitchen
table.
                    MARIA
          I've had enough of
          this! I've had enough!

TOM and JACQUES run into the kitchen.

                    JACQUES
          What the heck? (to
          MARIA) What's the
          matter?
```

You can find all the details of current North American film script formatting, cleverly written in the form of a script, at oscars.org /awards/nicholl/scriptsample.pdf.

The average script is 120 pages long, with each page roughly corresponding to one minute of screen time. Scripts can be a little shorter than this, but commercial scripts that run to 130 or 140 pages tend to be viewed as unprofessional in the industry. (Film auteurs, of course, can make their scripts whatever length they choose.)

Even if you're only doing a copy edit, it's worth reading some film scripts first. Some are published in hard copy; others—Casablanca, for example—can be found online. Some of these will be shooting scripts and will therefore include camera directions and possibly more extensive descriptions of characters and settings than are required in a script a writer will submit to a production company.

If you want to learn more about screenwriting and the substantive side of writing plays, books on these topics abound. The two listed below are considered classics of the genre:

Egri, Lajos. *The Art of Dramatic Writing: Its Basis in the Creative Interpretation of Human Motives.* New York: Simon & Schuster, 2004.

McKee, Robert. *Story: Substance, Structure, Style, and the Principles of Screenwriting.* New York: HarperCollins, 2012.

13.7 Cookbooks

13.7.1 Overview

If you can't cook, please skip this section and go edit something else. To edit recipes or a cookbook well, it helps to be as good a cook as you are an editor. While your mandate may not be to actually prepare the recipes to check for accuracy, if you know your way around a kitchen and understand culinary basics, you can at least suggest to an author that his roast chicken might take a little longer to cook than the 15 minutes stated in the recipe.

A good recipe editor might suggest an alternative utensil for certain steps (a whisk is better than a spatula for combining dry ingredients for a cake) or encourage a chef to streamline the steps in her recipe so it doesn't require readers to use every saucepan they possess.

As with most editing, wrangling recipes is a balancing act. In the case of a cookbook, the editor must weigh the author's ambitions, voice, and style of cooking with the readers' need for accurate, easy-to-understand recipes. After all, if you can't cook from a cookbook, what real use is it?

13.7.2 Recipe titles

These should be descriptive without being overly cute (unless the book is aimed at children).

The title should accurately reflect the recipe, so check that the recipe for Daube of Beef with Orange contains orange and that the Quick Couscous-Stuffed Peppers are, indeed, quick.

13.7.3 Recipe introductions

Recipe introductions (sometimes called headnotes or blurbs) aren't essential but are preferable. Ideally, they entice the reader to cook the recipe. If some recipes include an introduction, for consistency's sake all in the book should have one. The exceptions are basic recipes (e.g., stock), referenced throughout the book, that might be corralled in their own chapter toward the back.

Recipe introductions should not be boring but worth reading and informative. Avoid clichés. Simply stating the recipe is delicious/tasty/yummy doesn't cut it. (If the recipe isn't delicious/tasty/yummy, why is it in the book?) Avoid references to a recipe being the "definitive" version; there are myriad variations of every dish that's ever been cooked.

A good recipe introduction could include some combination of the following:

- details of the recipe's provenance or ethnicity
- the author's personal anecdote about the dish
- descriptions of uncommon ingredients, plus alternatives if appropriate
- details of any less familiar utensils the reader might need
- preparation or storage tips
- make-ahead instructions
- ways to make the dish lower in fat or vegetarian, if appropriate
- good accompaniments to serve with it
- a wine pairing

Ensure the information in the introduction accurately reflects the recipe: a recipe touted by the author as being suitable for a quick weekday supper needs to be simple to prepare and speedy to cook.

13.7.4 Notes/sidebars

Depending on the book's design, some of the items listed in 13.7.3—e.g., information on unfamiliar ingredients or utensils, or make-ahead or fat-trimming instructions—might be better treated as a note or a sidebar. Ensure such elements are treated consistently throughout the book.

Other sidebar content might include cooking methods that are repeated in several recipes (e.g., roasting peppers, toasting nuts, peeling tomatoes). Include a sidebar explaining the particular method with the recipe where it first appears (or where space allows), then add cross-references throughout the book.

13.7.5 Servings/yield

(a) Depending on the author's or publisher's preference or the design of the book, the servings line may appear immediately under the recipe title, after the introduction, or at the end of the recipe. Either way, retain consistency of wording throughout the book:

Serves 6 *or* Makes 6 servings

(b) Ensure that the number of servings corresponds to the quantities of ingredients in the recipes: a meat-based chili containing just 1 lb (500 g) ground beef and 1 can of beans would be unlikely to serve 12 people. Similarly, make sure the numbers add up. Something's amiss when the recipe instructs to make 9 crêpes, then says to arrange 3 on each of 4 plates.

(c) Ensure the way the yield is worded makes sense. The yield of recipes for beverages, sauces, salad dressings, pickles, jams, etc., should be given as a volume:

Makes 3 cups (750 mL) *or* Makes three 1-pint (500 mL) jars

Some baking recipes, such as cookies, can take an approximate yield:

Makes about 30 cookies

Bars and squares should take an exact yield:

Makes 12 bars

(d) In the case of a chef-written work, unless the book is a textbook for culinary professionals, encourage the author to downscale recipes that yield large, restaurant-size quantities.

13.7.6 Measurements

(a) Most mainstream cookbooks in North America use standard cup, tablespoon, and teaspoon measures, plus inches for length and ounces and pounds for weight. Canadian cookbooks have tended to include metric equivalents. Nevertheless, the author, publisher, and editor should confer on whether to include metric measures. A few specialized cookbooks—mostly baking books—use weight (ounces, pounds, and/or grams) for many ingredients.

If metric measures are to be included, most cookbook publishers can provide the editor with a list of standard equivalents. Or consult Canadian cookbooks by respected authors and draw up your own metric-equivalents guide.

(b) Although sets of measuring spoons sold in cookware stores often include an ⅛ teaspoon measure, many publishers prefer to substitute "a pinch" (for dry ingredients) or "a dash" (for wet ingredients).

(c) All ingredients listed should include a measure. Exceptions are salt, pepper, and other seasonings added according to taste, and garnishes:

Kosher salt and freshly ground black pepper to taste

Granulated sugar to taste

Shredded fresh basil leaves for garnish

Lemon wedges to serve

(d) Use common sense when matching a measure to an ingredient, remembering that most North American home cooks don't own a kitchen scale:

½ cup (125 mL) shredded cheddar cheese

✗ 2 oz (50 g) cheddar cheese, shredded

(e) Specifying the weight of an ingredient works best when the ingredient is purchased that way, but always consider what is easiest for the reader:

1 lb (500 g) ground chicken

✗ 4 cups (1 L) ground chicken

but, in a recipe for 4 people:

4 bone-in pork loin chops (about 8 oz/250 g each)

✗ 2 lb (1 kg) bone-in pork loin chops

(f) When a whole can or package of an ingredient is needed, specify the size most commonly available in grocery stores. When a partial package of an ingredient is used, it's better to specify an exact measure:

1½ cups (375 mL) canned diced tomatoes

✗ ½ can (28 oz/796 mL) diced tomatoes

13.7.7 Ingredients

(a) With the exception of unspecified amounts of water for, say, cooking pasta or vegetables, all the ingredients required for the recipe should be listed. Always ensure that the ingredients listed appear in the method and vice versa.

(b) Ingredients must be listed in the order in which they're used in the method:

Ingredients: 2 tbsp (30 mL) olive oil

3 cups (750 mL) sliced cremini mushrooms

Method: In a large skillet, heat oil over medium-high heat. Add mushrooms and cook, stirring …

(c) Generally, when two or more ingredients are used at the same time, list them in descending order of quantity. When two ingredients are used at the same time and have the same measure, list dry ingredients before wet:

2 tbsp (30 mL) ground coffee

1 tbsp (15 mL) chili powder

1 tbsp (15 mL) olive oil

1 tsp (5 mL) ground cumin

1 tsp (5 mL) minced garlic

An exception to the descending-order-of-quantity rule is when both citrus zest and juice are added to a recipe simultaneously, since the zest is grated before the fruit is squeezed of juice:

1 tsp (5 mL) grated lemon zest

2 tbsp (30 mL) lemon juice

(d) In a lengthy recipe, it can be helpful to the reader if the ingredients are divided by subheads, with the method following the same order and referencing the same subheads:

Ingredients:	Seared Scallops:
	Salad Greens:
	Vinaigrette:
Method:	For the seared scallops, ...
	For the salad greens, ...
	For the vinaigrette, ...

Consider dividing very lengthy or complicated recipes that could be daunting to the reader into separate recipes.

(e) Don't list an ingredient more than once unless the ingredients are divided by subheads (e.g., in cake ingredients divided into "Cake," "Filling," and "Icing," it's okay to list different amounts of granulated sugar in all three). When there are no subheads, it's preferable to combine the amounts of a repeated ingredient and add the word "divided" to alert the reader that the whole quantity isn't added at once:

Ingredients:	3 tbsp (45 mL) olive oil, divided
Method:	In a large skillet, heat 2 tbsp (30 mL) olive oil over medium-high heat ...
	Add the remaining olive oil ...

(f) Ensure the wording of the ingredients makes sense, especially when using volume measures:

1 onion, finely chopped *or* 1 cup (250 mL) finely chopped onion

✗ 1 cup (250 mL) onion, finely chopped

(g) Note that "½ cup (125 mL) butter, melted" and "½ cup (125 mL) melted butter" yield slightly different quantities that might not wreck a savoury recipe but could be significant in a baking recipe. Similarly, "1 cup (250 mL) mushrooms, sliced" is not the same as "1 cup (250 mL) sliced mushrooms." If in doubt, query.

(h) The wording of the ingredients list should be as exact as possible. Just a few of the questions you might need to ask an author include these:

- Are the chicken breasts boneless or bone-in? Are they skinless?
- Are the fish fillets skin-on or skinless?
- Is the butter salted or unsalted?
- Is the butter cold, softened, or melted?
- Is the salt kosher, sea, or table?
- Are the herbs dried or fresh?
- Is the cream whipping, table, or half-and-half?
- Are the potatoes peeled or not?
- Are the beans canned or dried, or green?
- Are the bread crumbs dry or soft/fresh?
- Is the sugar granulated, icing, or brown? If brown, is it light or dark?

(i) It's helpful to the reader to include the size of vegetables and fruits used:

> 1 large onion, chopped
>
> 2 medium apples, peeled, cored, and chopped

(j) If an ingredient requires a simple preparation before being used in the method, this information can be included in the ingredients list:

> 1 can (19 oz/540 mL) red kidney beans, drained and rinsed
>
> 2 pork chops, trimmed of excess fat
>
> 3 sweet potatoes, peeled and diced

Avoid lengthy preparation instructions that might run onto several lines of the ingredients list; these are better included in the method. (Make sure you rearrange the ingredients list if necessary.)

(k) Ensure consistency in wording. For example, does the author prefer "coriander" or "cilantro"? "Fresh ginger" or "ginger-root"? "Celery stalks" or "celery ribs"? "X cloves garlic" or "X garlic cloves"?

(l) Ingredients that could be omitted without compromising the recipe (a last-minute garnish, for example) should be followed by the word **optional** in parentheses:

> 2 tbsp (30 mL) shredded fresh basil (optional)

Depending on the publisher's style guide, the wording of the method might include **if using** (preceded by a comma) after the optional ingredient:

> Add basil, if using.

13.7.8 Method

(a) Always assume the reader knows very little about food and cooking. A well-written and well-edited recipe method should tell readers everything they need to know to prepare the recipe successfully.

(b) Choose verbs carefully to ensure they're appropriate for the action: "whisk" dry ingredients together for a cake, "scrape" cake batter into a baking pan, "toss" salad greens to combine. "Add" is sometimes clear, but often more descriptive terms are more helpful to the reader: "stir in," "fold in," "beat in," "pour in," etc.

(c) When editing a chef's recipes, watch for technical terms (chiffonade, julienne, reduction, deglaze, etc.) that may not be familiar to a general audience. Unless the book is specifically for culinary professionals or other experienced cooks, encourage the author to use more familiar terms or at least include definitions of technical terms.

(d) Tell the reader to preheat the oven, barbecue, or broiler at a point that makes sense in the method—at the beginning of the method if the appliance is to be used within 20 or 30 minutes, later on in the method if ingredients to be cooked need to be chilled or marinated first.

(e) For a recipe in which the position of the oven racks is important, include an instruction for adjusting their position along with the preheating instruction.

(f) Always specify the size of saucepan, skillet, baking dish, baking pan, bowl (whether for serving or prepping), etc. Say whether a baking sheet should be rimmed (for a recipe that might produce liquid that could drip onto the floor of the oven) or rimless (for, say, cookies).

(g) Specify whether baking pans are ungreased, greased, greased and floured, lined with parchment, etc.

(h) Specify whether a skillet is nonstick, ovenproof, or heavy based.

(i) Ensure a nonreactive saucepan or bowl is used with an acidic mixture.

(j) Always specify the heat over which an ingredient should be fried, sautéed, simmered, etc.

(k) Always specify whether the ingredient should be stirred constantly, stirred often, stirred occasionally, or left alone.

(l) If a step includes the instruction to simmer ingredients, specify whether the saucepan or skillet is covered, partially covered, or uncovered.

(m) Pay attention when a recipe says to "set aside" or "reserve" an ingredient or component. Make sure that item is not forgotten altogether.

(n) Always include both a cooking time and a watchpoint or doneness description:

> Add the onion and cook, stirring often, until the onion is softened but not browned, 5 to 7 minutes.

Bake for 30 minutes or until the top is golden brown and a tester inserted in the centre comes out clean.

The watchpoint for roast meat and poultry should refer to the appropriate internal temperature registered on a meat thermometer inserted into the thickest part of the meat and not touching any bone.

13.7.9 Nutrient analysis

Nutrient analysis of recipes, if required, should be done by a qualified dietitian. For the style and wording of analyses, consult with the publisher, author, or both and refer to other respected Canadian (or American, if appropriate) cookbooks with similar analyses.

For more information, refer to the websites of Health Canada (hc-sc.gc.ca), searching under "Food & Nutrition," or Dietitians of Canada (dietitians.ca).

13.7.10 Contents page/chapter headings

These come last because they're easier to pull together once an editor is familiar with the recipes in the book.

Is the book arranged by month or season? If so, do the recipes in each chapter make seasonal sense? A strawberry recipe in February or a heavy meat dish in the summer might not be such good ideas.

Likewise, are all the recipes in the appetizer chapter suitable for the task? Have any cake recipes crept into the cookie chapter?

Consider including a recipe listing at the start of each chapter as a service to the reader.

13.7.11 Index

The author or publisher should be encouraged to hire a qualified, experienced indexer. Many good cookbooks have been rendered second rate by inconsistent, inaccurate, or just plain sloppy indexing.

13.8 Magazines

Canada publishes a wide variety of magazines, in print and online, covering a spectrum of topics—from the technical, industrial, and scientific to the historical, literary, and artistic. The readership of many of these publications extends well beyond the nation's borders. That audience simultaneously reads a host of magazines and zines from other English-language sources. One online subscription service offers "over 100 of the world's top magazines," all of them in English. On that basis, Canadian magazines reflect a considerable degree of fluidity with respect to grammar, punctuation, syntax, and spelling, an approach consistent with the guiding principles of *Editing Canadian English*: "The goal is not to impose a uniform Canadian English style but to help editors make informed and appropriate choices for each project."

13.8.1 The global language

The importance of effective English in magazine publishing is underscored by the centrality of the language in world business and culture. English has become the lingua franca of the world, and about 80 percent of information stored in the world's computers is in English. Approximately two billion people use English as their native, second, business, or technical language.

The growth of English over the past millennium and past century has been dramatic. Old English (c. 450–1066) contained roughly 50,000 words; the first edition of the *Oxford English Dictionary* (1928) about 250,000. The English lexicon now contains more than a million words. Canadian writers and editors draw upon a vast and burgeoning English vocabulary to communicate with precision and clarity and to maximize the power of language to inform, entertain, and persuade.

13.8.1.1 *Canadianisms*

Canadian is a distinct form of English. Foreign readers of Canadian magazines may encounter the following Canadianisms: **chinook, chutes, muskeg, tamarack, Labrador tea, whisky jack, caribou, wendigo, inukshuk, mukluk, tuque, deke, spin-o-rama** (or **spinnerama**), **cannonading, Centre Hice** (whimsical definition of the initialism "CH" on Montreal Canadiens jerseys), poutine, **May 2-4 weekend, loonie, Timmy's** or **Timmys** (the latter mimicking the deleted possessive in "Hortons"), **Timbits,** and the incantatory **double-double,** to name a few, not to mention **biscuits** and **chesterfields.** A number of Canadian scholars have written voluminously about **eh,** both for and against its validity as a distinct Canadianism. Other "idiosyncrasies" such as the conversational tic **you know** ("yuh no") are prevalent throughout the English-speaking world.

13.8.1.2 *Canadian spelling*

Canadian spelling inhabits a middle ground between its British and American counterparts, a kind of bridge between their respective styles. (For a discussion of Canadian spelling and variants, see ECE3, chapter 3.) Canadian and British spellings share **apologize, centre, colour, cheque, convenor, dependant** (noun), **fibre, grey, instalment, licence** (noun), **mould, ochre, pyjamas,** and **theatre.** Canadian and American spellings share **airplane, aluminum, apnea, cozy, curb, generalize, initialize, orient** (verb), **tidbit,** and **tire.** Some words may be spelled the same in all three forms of English, among them **aesthetics, among, banister, cigarette, collectible, encyclopedia, focused, focusing, learned, wagon,** and **yogurt.**

Some characteristics of Canadian spelling may be more arresting to American readers than others—for example, the British practice of doubling consonants when adding **-ed** and **-ing** suffixes. American readers may pause at least momentarily at the Canadian spelling of **counselled** and **labelling,** but Canadian readers may not take issue with **counseled** and **labeling.** Here as elsewhere, the unique position of Canadian English, between the British and American models, affords opportunities to tailor house style to subject and audience/market. As a rule, it may be most prudent to choose spellings common to Canadian, British, and American English (e.g., **focused**). (For variant spellings by category, see ECE3, 3.5.)

As magazines are not normally audio publications, their publishers are seldom obliged to address the zee/zed schism and the use of the American pronunciation of that letter in a variety of **E-Z** and **LA-Z** products.

13.8.2 Advice for magazine writers and editors

The following recommendations, deriving from a scan of approximately 50 print and electronic magazines, may benefit writers and editors:

1. Avoid clichéd words and expressions. They bore readers and have the opposite of their intended effect. The soporific "world class" and "cutting edge" are examples.

2. Avoid nebulous buzzwords. The vague, exhausted "engage" may top this list.

3. Don't overload text with exclamation marks in an effort to create excitement.

4. Understand the differences among hyphens, en dashes, and em dashes. They are valuable punctuational tools. (For hyphenation, see ECE3, 4.8. For the en dash, see ECE3, 4.9.2.)

5. The use of three ellipsis points rather than four is always correct (see ECE3, 7.5). This choice saves a great deal of time and study. And it ensures consistency. Some designers prefer ellipses to be separated by single word spaces (. . .), resulting in a cleaner, more spacious feel to the page. It may be necessary to key ellipses individually, as some word processing programs provide a precomposed unspaced triple-dot symbol (...) as a default character.

6. Sometimes the passive voice is more powerful than the active, as when the desired emphasis is on the recipient rather than on the agent of an action (e.g., "Princess Diana was hounded by the paparazzi") or when the agent of the action is unknown (e.g., "The wheel was invented in prehistory"). The best writing mixes both voices.

7. Always use a serif font for extended text. In this context, it is both more legible and more aesthetically pleasing.

8. Use apostrophes ('), not single primes ('), for possessives. Use double quotation marks (" "), not double primes (" "), for quoted material, and use single quotation marks (' ') for quotes within quotations. For abbreviations of decades (e.g., **the '60s**), note that an apostrophe (not a single opening quotation mark) replaces the missing numerals. Note

carefully the "6," "9," "66," and "99," orientation of the punctuation. (For smart quotes vs. plain quotes, see ECE3, 7.6.4.)

9.   Don't shy away from an occasional long sentence. It is sometimes the best option. Length alone does not make a sentence "rambling." Respect the intelligence of your reader and don't try to dumb down. The key is to alternate sentence lengths.

10. Proofread, proofread, proofread. One of the most critical aspects of the publishing process is proofreading. Such scrutiny, preferably by a fresh pair of eyes, may preclude the transmission of unnecessary trivial—and sometimes glaring—errors. Such infelicities appear in the media with unfortunate frequency. One source in 2014 informed that by mid-winter the city of Windsor, Ontario, had already exacerbated its budget for snow removal.

13.9   Science, technology, and medicine

Many authors in Canadian academia, government, and industry place high value on editors who can understand scientific and technical material—and they pay accordingly. Some authors who are brilliant in their fields of expertise lack fluency in English, requiring superior levels of comprehension from their editors. Even when working with authors who write well, editors who do not understand the content of the manuscript can inadvertently change the meaning. They should always flag passages where the science is unclear to them or where their editing may have subverted the author's intent.

Documents in the many specialized fields of science, technology, and medicine normally target one of two audiences: peer groups who understand the jargon or members of the public who do not. For documents aimed at peer groups, editors should know enough of the jargon and conventions to avoid overediting. These editors should be able to catch factual and logical errors as well, which can require a knowledge level in the field equivalent to a BSc degree or higher. On the other hand, writers who wish to communicate complex concepts to general audiences may benefit from editors who are unfamiliar with the jargon.

13.9.1 Style guides and dictionaries

No comprehensive style guide has been published for Canadian science, technology, or medicine. However, editors may use a Canadian style guide such as this manual or *The Canadian Style* in combination with an area-specific scientific, technical, or medical style guide. Similarly, editors may use any of the standard Canadian dictionaries as a general reference together with field-specific dictionaries for the technical words. Always check with the author or publisher about which style guides and dictionaries to follow. Whenever possible, the most recent edition of a guide or dictionary should be used as a reference: science continues to advance, making the less current references less useful.

13.9.1.1 Science

Style guides: Major style guides in this category include the following:

- *Scientific Style and Format (The CSE Manual)*, published by the Council of Science Editors as a guide for the natural sciences.

- *The ACS Style Guide*, published by the American Chemical Society as a guide for chemistry, physics, and related disciplines.

- *Subtleties of Scientific Style*, an entertaining online handbook written by an experienced Australian science editor (science scape.com.au).

- *Mathematics into Type*, published online by the American Mathematical Society (https://www.ams.org/publications/authors/mit-2.pdf).

Some general style manuals also contain useful material on editing science. These include

- *The Chicago Manual of Style*, which has not only sections on scientific terminology, scientific abbreviations, and SI units but also entire chapters on illustrations, tables, and mathematics in type.

- The *Publication Manual of the American Psychological Association* (APA), which includes sections on style for SI units, figures, tables, and statistical and mathematical copy.

- The *New Oxford Style Manual*, which has a full chapter on editing science and mathematics.

Alternatively, many Canadian scientists follow the house styles of publishers or scholarly societies relevant to their disciplines. Style guides range from succinct "Instructions to Authors" Internet postings such as that of the American Institute of Physics (AIP style; publishing.aip.org/authors) to full-length Canadian style manuals such as *Geoscience Reporting Guidelines*.

Dictionaries: Useful science dictionaries include the *Oxford Dictionary of Science* and the *New Oxford Dictionary for Scientific Writers and Editors*. Also, many dictionaries covering specific fields of science are available in print and online.

13.9.1.2 *Technology*

The dominant industrial sectors of Canada—manufacturing, mining, petroleum, construction, forestry, agriculture, and various service sectors—require considerable amounts of documentation in engineering and information technology to support their continuing operations and their regulation by government.

Style guides: Engineers tend to use house styles based on one or more of the following sources:

- One of the scientific style guides listed in 13.9.1.1.

- A style guide from a Canadian or American journal in their branch of engineering.

- A style guide published by the relevant engineering society (often American). An example is the *IEEE Editorial Style Manual*, used widely by electrical and computer engineers in Canada (ieee.org/documents/style_manual.pdf).

In fields that see large numbers of American expatriates working in Canada (such as petroleum engineering), American spelling and style guides are often accepted and sometimes expected.

Technical writers in information technology also tend to follow American style guides, perhaps because of the pervasive influence of large U.S. companies in this field. Recent manuals include

- *Microsoft Manual of Style*, a large technical style manual with guidance on usage, style, voice, formatting, grammar, web content, globalization, accessibility, and emerging standards. It also has a usage dictionary of more than 1,000 technical terms and usage choices.

- *The IBM Style Guide*, a full-length computer industry guide on grammar, punctuation, formatting, document structure, and other computer-related style points.

- *The Yahoo! Style Guide*, a popular guide on writing and editing for an online audience.

- *IEEE Computer Society Style Guide 2016*, a detailed manual with a combined style sheet and glossary of computing terms (computer.org/portal/web/publications/styleguide).

Dictionaries: In addition to the dictionaries discussed in 13.9.1.1, editors of technical material may find comprehensive science and technology dictionaries useful:

- *McGraw-Hill Dictionary of Scientific and Technical Terms*

- *Chambers Dictionary of Science and Technology*

- *ASTM Dictionary of Engineering, Science, and Technology*

13.9.1.3   Medicine

Style guides: The *AMA Manual of Style*, published by the American Medical Association, is the pre-eminent North American style guide for medical editing. Canadian medical journals and publishing houses have their own style guides as well.

Dictionaries: Popular medical dictionaries include *Stedman's*, *Dorland's*, *Taber's*, *Mosby's*, and the *Oxford Concise Medical Dictionary*. The entries of the *Merriam-Webster's Medical Dictionary* are provided in the Merriam-Webster online dictionary as a separate tab (merriam-webster.com/medical/) and in the MedlinePlus online medical dictionary (https://medlineplus .gov/mplusdictionary.html).

Note that Canadian spelling in the field of medicine often allows both American and British spelling. For example, an author or publisher may require either "pediatrics" or "paediatrics" depending on the style guide and dictionary used.

13.9.2 Citations and references

Citations: Publications in some areas of science, technology, and medicine require a sequentially numbered endnote reference style known as the citation-sequence system. This style saves space, and word processing or reference management software can easily keep the numbers properly sequential during writing and editing. (For more on citations, see ECE3, chapter 9. For reference management software, see 9.7.)

Citation numbers may be distinguished from the body text by enclosing them in parentheses or brackets, as is the requirement in the journal *Science*:

> What Newton (74) was to physics, Lavoisier (75, 76) was to chemistry (80–82).

Some publishers require superscript citation numbers instead, some with spaces after the commas and some without. For example, the journal *Nature* uses superscripts with no spaces:

> What Newton[74] was to physics, Lavoisier[75,76] was to chemistry.[80–82]

The placement of superscript citation numbers requires extra care because scientific writing frequently includes numbers and units that can have exponents; for example, $G = 6.670 \times 10^{-11}$ N·m^2·kg^{-2}. Placing a superscript citation number immediately after any numbers or units may result in ambiguity. Therefore, most scientific style guides require that superscript citation numbers must follow all punctuation marks (except the dash) and never immediately follow a number or unit.

Many publishers in science and technology prefer brief reference styles that minimize punctuation marks and use abbreviated titles of journals and conference proceedings. Extensive lists of such abbreviations are available from the Chemical Abstracts Service (cassi.cas.org/search.jsp) and the U.S. National Library of Medicine (ncbi.nlm.nih.gov/nlmcatalog/journals). Medical writers now tend to favour the ultracompact Vancouver system of citation. The U.S. National Library of Medicine has published a comprehensive version of this system online: *Citing Medicine: The NLM Guide for Authors, Editors, and Publishers* (nlm.nih.gov /citingmedicine). AMA style is based on this standard.

Most academic authors have personal databases of references and use citation software such as EndNote or Reference Manager (for a discussion of reference management software, see ECE3, 9.7). However, if authors have incorrectly or incompletely populated some of the fields in their databases, the software will not correctly format the affected references. Bibliographies still need to be edited, but editors should take care not to change the field codes inserted by the software.

13.9.3 SI units

Editors in science, technology, and medicine must have a thorough knowledge of the International System of Units (SI). For a discussion and examples of SI, see ECE3, 8.1.

Some industries and fields of study do not fully embrace SI and still allow some use of traditional units and styles. Editors in these fields will need to be aware of the expected usages.

13.9.4 Font-related problems

13.9.4.1 *Substitution of incorrect characters by authors*

Standard Unicode fonts such as Times New Roman contain almost all the special characters and symbols needed in scientific publications. However, authors sometimes substitute other characters that approximate the desired symbol. Table 13.4 provides a list of such characters and their hexadecimal Unicode numbers of the correct characters.

To enter the correct character in a Microsoft Word document using these numbers in Windows systems,

1. Type a space (if directly following a number in the text).

2. Type in the hexadecimal Unicode number of the character (letters are not case-sensitive).

3. Hold down the Alt key and type an "x".

In Mac systems, the behaviour of the Option key must first be set to enable Unicode hexadecimal input:

1. Go to the System Preferences menu, look under the Keyboard item, and ensure that the box next to "Show Keyboard & Character Viewers in menu bar" is checked.

2. Next to that, click on "Input Sources" (or go to the Language & Text preference pane and choose "Input Sources") and select the keyboard layout "Unicode Hex Input". Also make sure that "Show Input menu in menu bar" is checked.

Thereafter, the correct character may be entered as follows:

1. Click on the flag icon in the menu bar and choose "Unicode Hex Input".

2. Hold down the Option (or Alt) key and enter the hexadecimal Unicode number of the character. Release the Option key.

To return the Option key to its normal functions, click on the flag icon and choose the normal input method.

Inputting Unicode numbers on Mac systems allows the use of symbols that cannot be accessed with standard Mac keyboard shortcuts, and it can be more convenient than using the Mac Character Viewer if the desired codes are already known to the writer.

Note that Unicode text fonts do not include all specialized scientific characters, and a different font may sometimes be substituted. The Unicode Consortium has posted the full set of Unicode character charts online (unicode.org/charts).

Table 13.4   Common scientific symbols vulnerable to substitution

Correct character	Unicode number (hexa-decimal)	Possible incorrect substitutions
Minus sign (−)	2212	Hyphen (-) or en dash (–)
Multiplication sign (×)	00D7	Letter x or X or Greek letter chi (X or χ)
Middle dot for multiplication of units (·)	00B7	Bullet (•), period (.), or superscript period (˙)
Multiplication asterisk (∗) used in computing	2217[a]	Normal raised asterisk (*)
Double hyphen (--) used in computer code	002D (twice)	Em dash (—)
Micro sign (μ) or Greek small letter mu (μ)	00B5; 03BC	Letter u or Greek small letter upsilon (υ)
Degree sign (°)	00B0	Masculine ordinal indicator (º), ring above (˚), superscript letter o (ᵒ) or O (ᴼ), or superscript zero (⁰)
Greater-than-or-equal-to sign (≥)	2265	Greater-than sign with added underlining (≥)
Less-than-or-equal-to sign (≤)	2264	Less-than sign with added underlining (≤)
Plus-minus sign (±)	00B1	Plus sign with added underlining (±)
Straight apostrophe (') used in computer code	0027	Right or left single quotation mark (' or ')
Prime symbol or unit symbol for plane angle minutes (′)	2032	Straight apostrophe ('), acute accent (´), or closing single curly quotation mark (')

[a] May not be available in normal Unicode text fonts such as Times New Roman.

Table 13.4 (continued)

Correct character	Unicode number (hexa-decimal)	Possible incorrect substitutions
Double prime symbol or unit symbol for plane angle seconds (″)	2033	Straight quotation mark ("), double acute accent (″), closing double curly quotation mark (") or two single primes (″)
Straight quotation mark (") used in computer code	0022	Opening or closing double curly quotation mark (" or ") or two straight apostrophes (")
Partial differential operator (∂)	2202	Greek letter delta (δ)
Proportional sign (∝)	221D[a]	Greek letter alpha (α)
Greek letter beta (β)	03B2	Letter B or German letter "sharp s" (ß)
Greek letter eta (η)	03B7	Letter n
Greek letter kappa (κ)	03BA	Letter k or K
Greek letter nu (ν); italics nu (ν)	03BD	Letter v, italics letter v, Greek letter upsilon (υ), or italics upsilon (υ)
Greek letter rho (ρ)	03C1	Letter p or P
Number zero (0)	0030	Letter o or O or Greek letter omicron (o or O)
Number one (1)	0031	Letter l or I (especially in sans serif fonts)

[a] May not be available in normal Unicode text fonts such as Times New Roman.

The Chicago Manual gives other examples of potentially ambiguous symbols and characters in the chapter on mathematics in type.

13.9.4.2 *Substitution of incorrect characters by computers*

Authors and publishers sometimes use different fonts for symbols and normal text, but this can result in uneven line heights and obvious differences in typographic style. Furthermore, the computers of the author, the editor, and the publisher may not have the same symbol fonts installed. If the author uses an unusual symbol font to insert special characters, other computers may substitute another font that does not map onto the correct character. This font mapping problem can result in blank spaces or small empty box symbols where the symbols should appear. In the worst cases, major errors or misunderstandings can result. For example, "μ" in a symbol font sometimes maps onto "m" in the substitute font. Therefore, units of μm (micrometres) can change to units of mm (millimetres)—a thousandfold error. Editors should ensure that Greek letters and other special symbols are set either in the same font as the surrounding text or in a specific symbol font approved by the publisher.

Capitalization, roman type, italics, superscripts, and subscripts all may have specific meanings in scientific text. Editors must watch carefully for errors and inconsistencies of font usage in scientific symbols. The autocorrect features of word processing software may also cause errors. For example, most computer languages use characters such as straight apostrophes and straight quotation marks for specific coding purposes; therefore, autocorrection to curly single or double quotation marks will likely cause the affected code to fail. Some computer languages are also case-sensitive, so autocorrecting the case may change the outcome.

13.9.5 Equations

The term "equation" in publishing usually includes mathematical expressions, chemical reactions, and other types of expressions using symbols. Authors can place equations either on a separate line (display equations) or within the body of the text (in-line equations). *The Chicago Manual* and *Mathematics into Type* (https://www.ams.org/publications/authors/mit-2.pdf) provide further details about typesetting, numbering, and punctuating such expressions.

For specialized software used to typeset equations, chemical reactions, and equation-format diagrams, see 12.6.3.2.

Authors frequently mishandle the spacing within mathematical expressions. If a binary operator (such as =, +, $\geq$, or $\pm$) functions as a verb or a conjunction, then the expression requires a space on both sides of the operator; for example, $n = 10$ or $x + y$. Standard abbreviations for mathematical functions set in roman type (for example, log, exp, and sin) also require spaces on both sides, unless the argument of the function is enclosed in "fences" (parentheses, brackets, or braces); for example, 2 log x, but 2 log$(x + y)$. In-line mathematical expressions should be short and contain only non-breaking spaces.

In superscripts and subscripts, however, all spaces should be removed unless ambiguity results (e.g., e^{x+y} and $\Delta H^{25°C}$). In mathematical expressions, do not put spaces on either side of slashes (x/y), middle dots $(x \cdot y^{-1})$, or colons used to indicate ratios (e.g., a 2:1 ratio). When an operator functions as an adjective (i.e., as a modifier of just a single number), then do not insert a space between the operator and the number; for example, 100× magnification and a probability of >95% (but $p > 95\%$). *Mathematics into Type* presents further details.

Editors should always query authors about mathematically ambiguous double divisors (for example, m·kg/s³/A) and substitute an unambiguous form using either a single divisor with appropriate parentheses [m·kg/(s³·A)] or exponents (m·kg·s⁻³·A⁻¹).

The choice of font can affect the meaning of mathematical symbols. ISO 80000 style includes the following rules:

- Use roman type for units, numerals, mathematical constants (π or e), mathematical operators and functions with fixed meanings (d for derivative or cos for cosine), chemical formulas, punctuation, and descriptive terms (min for minimum).

- Use italics for single-letter symbols that represent physical quantities or variables, whether they are known (the speed of light c) or unknown (mass m). Italics are also used for symbols representing user-definable functions and operators [the function $f(x)$]. Note that other styles may prohibit this italicization of physical constants and Greek letters. Furthermore, multi-letter variable symbols for variables are sometimes set in roman type to avoid confusion with multiple single-letter variables (e.g., IP instead of IP for ionization potential).

- Use boldface type for tensors, matrices, and multidimensional quantities. Vectors are sometimes represented in print by boldface italic letters.

These rules apply within superscripts and subscripts as well. For example, in the standard symbol for chemical activation energy, E_a, the italic E is a variable representing a quantity of energy and the subscript roman "a" is just a descriptive label standing for activation.

Each field has its own rules and conventions for the typography of its specialized symbols. For further information, see the style guides listed in 13.9.1.

13.9.6 Tables

Editors in science and technology should know how to use the Microsoft Word tools for constructing and formatting tables, because some authors will still construct tables using the tab key and the space bar.

Tables should have a clear purpose and a logical and consistent organization. Table design should be as simple and clutter-free as possible. (Long lists that are presented in multiple columns may be handled either as figures or as informal tables without table numbering.)

Wherever possible, editors should verify the content of each table at least for logic and consistency. Checking sums may result in good catches.

The Chicago Manual and the major style guides listed in 13.9.1 provide additional details and many examples. Other useful references include *Presenting Numbers, Tables, and Charts* and *The Chicago Guide to Writing about Numbers*.

13.9.7 Figures

The best scientific figures have a clear and simple design with no extra clutter: in general, avoid colours, patterns, grid lines, and special backgrounds.

All text placed within figures should follow the same rules as the body text regarding units, symbols, and mathematical expressions. Editors should also check the content of the figures for correctness or at least plausibility.

Editors often have only three options for editing figures:

- Have the figures converted into PDF files and use PDF editing software to mark them up (see 12.6.4).

- Mark up printouts of the figures by hand and scan the marked-up pages for the author.

- Simply compile a list of comments for the author.

Print publications almost universally require authors to submit figures electronically. Authors must normally submit line art (charts, diagrams, and maps) in a vector file format, because it allows publishers to scale up images without losing detail. All other types of figures—such as scans, digital photographs, and half-tone illustrations—must be submitted in a raster image format. Such images become pixelated when scaled up, so publishers usually specify a minimum level of resolution.

Note that EPS and PDF files can contain both vector and raster image data. Publishers may accept PDF files for either print or web publications, but the file specifications will differ depending on the medium.

Internet publications may prefer to receive figures as smaller GIF, JPEG, or PNG raster image files.

The *Chicago Manual* and the style guides listed in 13.9.1 and 13.9.6 present further information on editing figures. Another resource is *The Wall Street Journal Guide to Information Graphics*.

13.9.8 Compatibility of file types

Most editors now use Microsoft Word or Word-compatible systems such as LibreOffice and Apache OpenOffice. However, incomplete compatibility between software systems may cause problems for authors and editors, especially in documents containing equations and special symbols. (For a discussion of how font substitution can change meanings, see 13.9.4.2.)

Problems can also occur between versions of the same software. For example, saving a Word .docx file as a Word .doc file can remove features from the file that will remain lost, even if the .doc file is then reopened in a Word version that supports .docx files.

If the author and editor use different word processing systems or different versions of the same system, the editor may wish to ask for a hard copy or a PDF version of the file and check for errors caused by file incompatibilities.

13.9.9 Editing LaTeX documents

Mathematicians, computing scientists, physicists, and engineers in related areas have used the LaTeX typesetting system for decades. LaTeX (pronounced "lay-tek" or "lah-tek") allows authors to set complex equations perfectly and enables easy conversions of documents to other formatting styles and file types, including HTML. Some major publishers in these fields encourage authors to submit their works in LaTeX because it simplifies their publishing process. LaTeX resembles HTML in that it is freely available and it compiles plain-text files marked up with formatting tags; however, it can also be dauntingly complex and unforgiving of seemingly trivial errors in coding. The LaTeX community has thus developed a variety of tools to make LaTeX easier to use.

LaTeX files may be edited in several ways:

- Import the plain-text LaTeX source file into a free LaTeX document processor such as LyX (pronounced "lix"; lyx.org), which enforces correct LaTeX syntax, makes editing easier, and allows the tracking of changes.

- Import the plain-text LaTeX source file into Word (complete with tags) and track the changes in Word. The author can then accept or reject changes, save the edited Word file as plain text, and recompile using LaTeX. However, the author will have to check for coding errors introduced by the editor or by Word.

- Obtain a Word-compatible output file (without tags) from the author and edit this file in Word, tracking the changes. The author can then copy and paste the desired changes from the edited Word file into the LaTeX source code, checking for coding errors as above.

- Obtain a PDF output file from the author and mark up this file using PDF editing software (see 12.6.4). Depending on the type of markup applied, the author may have to transfer the edits without the benefit of copy and paste.

To avoid introducing coding errors, editors should turn off all autocorrect functions and take into account the idiosyncrasies of LaTeX. For example, LaTeX reserves certain keyboard characters for coding purposes (including \, &, $, {, }, %, #, ^, and _). Other keyboard characters may function differently than expected or work properly only in particular LaTeX modes.

For a comprehensive LaTeX symbol list, see ctan.org/pkg /comprehensive.

13.9.10 Editing HTML and XML documents

Large numbers of scientific and technical documents are posted online as HTML and XML files. Editors may work with these files using methods analogous to those outlined for editing LaTeX files (see 13.9.9).

Note that using the "save as HTML" functions of word processing software such as Word may introduce undesired code and disrupt the intended formatting of the web page. Editors also should turn off all autocorrect functions.

To display scientific symbols properly in a browser (including certain keyboard characters such as < and >), HTML and XML use short predefined strings of code called character references.

Two types of character references exist for many symbols:

- numeric character references, which use predefined decimal or hexadecimal numbers

- character entity references ("entities" for short), which use more intuitive predefined strings of letters

Each character reference always begins with an ampersand and ends with a semicolon. For example, an editor needing a greater-than (>) symbol in the output text should insert either the corresponding entity (>), the decimal numeric character reference (>), or the hexadecimal numeric character reference (>). Current lists of entities and numeric character references may be found online (e.g., from webdesign.about.com /library/bl_htmlcodes.htm).

13.9.11 Additional considerations for proposals and reports

Large numbers of works in science, technology, and medicine are not intended for publication or will see only limited distribution. Proposals and reports constitute the two major categories of such documents.

13.9.11.1 Proposals

Proposals may be applications for research funding or responses to requests for proposals (RFPs) to provide technical goods or services. Often written within the framework of a competition, proposals are normally confidential. Editors who understand the review process and cater to the needs of the review committee can increase the chances of success in the competition. Good proposals will have uncluttered and easy-to-read designs.

For all types of competitive proposals, editors should ensure that the submitted documents closely follow the rules of the competition. Failure to do so can result in truncation or rejection of the proposal by administrative staff.

Draft proposals often exceed the specified length limits, so editors must have sufficient understanding of the topic to be able to reduce the length without cutting essential content. Using shorthand terms and jargon sometimes helps, but too many acronyms can reduce reader comprehension and may annoy the reviewers.

On the other hand, some audiences will be comfortable with the use of science and technology terms such as DNA or HTML.

Canadian granting agencies and RFP-issuing organizations generally expect to see Canadian style and spelling in the proposals submitted to them.

13.9.11.2 Reports

Technical reports vary greatly in their complexity, purpose, and confidentiality. Examples include reports of technical results to a client, research grant reports to funding agencies, environmental compliance reports to regulatory agencies, reports of government technical committees, and white papers used for business-to-business marketing in a technical field. All offer opportunities for editors, but research and technical reports are often edited in-house because of confidentiality concerns. *The Canadian Style* offers a useful section on report writing and editing.

For further reading

General style guides

The Canadian Style: A Guide to Writing and Editing. Revised and expanded. Toronto: Dundurn Press in cooperation with Public Works and Government Services Canada Translation Bureau, 1997. [312 pp.] btb.termiumplus.gc.ca.

The Chicago Manual of Style: The Essential Guide for Writers, Editors, and Publishers. 16th ed. Chicago: University of Chicago Press, 2010. [1026 pp.] chicagomanualofstyle.org.

Science style guides

The ACS Style Guide: Effective Communication of Scientific Information. 3rd ed. Edited by Anne M. Coghill and Lorrin R. Garson. Washington, DC: American Chemical Society; New York: Oxford University Press, 2006. [430 pp.]

AIP Publishing. "Author Resource Guide." American Institute of Physics. [21 pp.] http://publishing.aip.org/authors.

Grant, B. *Geoscience Reporting Guidelines*. Victoria, BC: privately published, 2003. [356 pp.] https://www.gac.ca/publications /view_pub.php?id=54.

New Oxford Style Manual. 2nd ed. New York: Oxford University Press, 2012. [880 pp.]

Publication Manual of the American Psychological Association. 6th ed. Washington, DC: American Psychological Association, 2009. [272 pp.]

Scientific Style and Format: The CSE Manual for Authors, Editors, and Publishers. 8th ed. Reston, VA: Council of Science Editors, 2014. [840 pp.] scientificstyleandformat.org.

Stevens, Matthew. *Subtleties of Scientific Style*. Thornleigh, Australia: ScienceScape Editing, 2007. [103 pp.] sciencescape .com.au.

Swanson, Ellen. *Mathematics into Type*. Updated edition by Arlene O'Sean and Antoinette Schleyer. Providence, RI: American Mathematical Society, 1999. [102 pp.] https://www.ams.org/ publications/authors/mit-2.pdf.

Science dictionaries

Oxford Dictionary of Science. 6th ed. Edited by Elizabeth A. Martin. Oxford: Oxford University Press, 2010. [912 pp.]

The New Oxford Dictionary for Scientific Writers and Editors. 2nd ed. Edited by Alan Isaacs, John Daintith, and Elizabeth Martin. Oxford: Oxford University Press, 2009. [464 pp.]

Technology style guides

DeRespinis, Francis, Peter Hayward, Jana Jenkins, Amy Laird, Leslie McDonald, and Eric Radzinski. *The IBM Style Guide: Conventions for Writers and Editors*. Upper Saddle River, NJ: IBM Press/Pearson, 2011. [381+ pp.]

IEEE Computer Society Style Guide 2016. Washington, DC: IEEE Computer Society, 2016. [105 pp.] computer.org/portal/web/ publications/styleguide.

IEEE Editorial Style Manual. Piscataway, NJ: Institute of Electrical and Electronics Engineers, 2014. [18 pp.] https://www.ieee.org/documents/style_manual.pdf.

Microsoft Manual of Style: Your Everyday Guide to Usage, Terminology, and Style for Professional Technical Communications. 4th ed. Redmond, WA: Microsoft Press, 2012. [438 pp.]

The Yahoo! Style Guide: The Ultimate Sourcebook for Writing, Editing, and Creating Content for the Digital World. Edited by Chris Barr. New York: Yahoo! Inc. and St. Martin's Griffin, 2010. [528 pp.]

Technology dictionaries

ASTM Dictionary of Engineering, Science, and Technology. 10th ed. West Conshohocken, PA: ASTM International, 2005. [670 pp.]

Chambers Dictionary of Science and Technology. Edited by John Lackie. London: Chambers, 2007. [1364 pp.]

McGraw-Hill Dictionary of Scientific and Technical Terms. 6th ed. Edited by Sybil P. Parker. New York: McGraw-Hill, 2003. [2380 pp.] [The 7th edition is scheduled for release in 2016.]

Medical style guides

AMA Manual of Style: A Guide for Authors and Editors. 10th ed. New York: American Medical Association and Oxford University Press, 2007. [1010 pp.]

Medical dictionaries

Dorland's Illustrated Medical Dictionary. 32nd ed. Philadelphia: Elsevier Saunders, 2012. [2176 pp.]

MedlinePlus. *Medical Dictionary.* U.S. National Library of Medicine. https://medlineplus.gov/mplusdictionary.html.

Merriam-Webster. *Medical Dictionary* [tab on web page]. https://www.merriam-webster.com/medical.

Merriam-Webster's Medical Dictionary. Springfield, MA: Merriam-Webster, 2006. [833 pp.]

Mosby's Medical Dictionary, 9th ed. St. Louis, MO: Elsevier/ Mosby, 2013. [1984 pp.]

Oxford Concise Medical Dictionary. 8th ed. Oxford: Oxford University Press, 2010. [840 pp.]

Stedman's Medical Dictionary. 28th ed. Baltimore: Lippincott Williams & Wilkins, 2005. [2100 pp.]

Taber's Cyclopedic Medical Dictionary, 22nd ed. Philadelphia: F.A. Davis, 2013. [2880 pp.]

Citations and references

American Chemical Society. "CAS Source Index (CASSI) Search Tool." 2014. http://cassi.cas.org/search.jsp.

Patrias, Karen. *Citing Medicine: The NLM Guide for Authors, Editors, and Publishers.* 2nd ed. Technical editor Dan Wendling. Bethesda, MD: National Library of Medicine, 2007. [Online; updated 2015]. https://www.ncbi.nlm.nih.gov/books/NBK7256.

U.S. National Library of Medicine, National Center for Biotechnology Information. "NLM Catalog: Journals Referenced in the NCBI Databases." 2014. ncbi.nlm.nih.gov /nlmcatalog/journals.

Special characters and mathematical equations

ISO 80000-1:2009. *Quantities and Units — Part 1: General.* Geneva: International Organization for Standardization, 2009. iso.org.

Swanson, Ellen. *Mathematics into Type.* Updated edition by Arlene O'Sean and Antoinette Schleyer. Providence, RI: American Mathematical Society, 1999. [102 pp.] ncbi.nlm.nih. gov/nlmcatalog/journals.

Unicode, Inc. "Unicode 7.0 Character Code Charts." unicode.org /charts.

Tables and figures

Bigwood, Sally, and Melissa Spore. *Presenting Numbers, Tables, and Charts.* Oxford: Oxford University Press, 2003. [144 pp.]

Miller, Jane E. *The Chicago Guide to Writing about Numbers: The Effective Presentation of Quantitative Information.* Chicago: University of Chicago Press, 2004. [304 pp.]

Wong, Dona M. *The Wall Street Journal Guide to Information Graphics: The Dos and Don'ts of Presenting Data, Facts, and Figures.* New York: W.W. Norton, 2010. [160 pp.]

LaTeX, HTML, and XML documents

Jeremy Girard. "HTML Codes and Special Characters, 2017." https://www.thoughtco.com/html-codes-special-characters-4061089.

Pakin, Scott. "The Comprehensive LaTeX Symbol List." Comprehensive TeX Archive Network (CTAN), 2009. https://ctan.org/pkg/comprehensive.

"XML Entity Definitions for Characters (2nd Edition)." World Wide Web Consortium (W3C), 2014. https://www.w3.org/TR/xml-entity-names.

13.10 Visual materials

Visual materials can take many different forms. Each type of visual comes with its own set of editorial considerations.

(a) Visual material is essentially any material that is not part of the main text or a block quote. It may require special formatting and it may be text-based or image-based. On the page, visual material stands out.

(b) Text-based visuals usually take the form of lists or tables. Both require special formatting and have their own editorial considerations. Lists may be bulleted, numbered, or unnumbered. In some cases, lists are "run in" with the main text; in other cases, they are visibly separate. (For more on lists, see 13.10.5.1.) Tables consist of two or more columns that present data sets in a manner that simplifies comparison.

(c) Image-based visuals are more diverse in nature. Charts and graphs are two forms of image-based visual material, and there are many variations. They commonly convey numeric data. Like tables, graphs and charts usually facilitate comparison. (For more on charts and graphs, see 13.10.5.2.)

(d) Figures may be similar to graphs or charts, or may take the form of diagrams. Some diagrams are very detailed, such as those in laboratory manuals; others may be simpler. "Line art" figures may likewise be simple or complex. A simple piece of line art may be an outline of a shape, while a more complicated piece of line art might show the correct method for wearing safety glasses. A technical illustration is a specialized diagram that shows, in great detail, the various parts and specifications of a piece of equipment. Technical illustrations are most common in fields that use, design, or manufacture parts for mechanized devices, although they may appear in other publications. (For more on technical illustrations, see 13.10.5.5.) A map is another specialized form of diagram, which conveys geographic information. (For more on maps, see 13.10.5.6.)

(e) Other image-based visual materials are photographs and reproductions of works of fine art, such as paintings, or other artwork. (For more on photographs, see 13.10.5.3.) In some cases, these types of visual material may be referred to as illustrations. The term "illustration" usually refers to drawings, such as the images that appear in children's picture books or cartoons and comics. Some publications, such as graphic novels and comic books, are focused on illustrations, whereas others may have no illustrations at all. (For more on illustrations, see 13.10.5.4.)

13.10.1 Range in function of visuals

(a) Visuals serve a number of purposes in a publication. The most common reason to include visual material is to inform the reader. Most visual material conveys complicated information in a format that is more readily accessible. For example, a list may offer the most salient points of a complicated scientific study, or a table may present data in a form that is clearer than if it were written out.

(b) Tables, lists, graphs, charts, maps, technical illustrations, and diagrams/line art are usually considered "informative." Photographs and reproductions of works of art may help illustrate the text's argument, or eliminate the need for a wordy description of the image. Illustrations may also elaborate on the text. This is especially true in children's books, where text tends to be more sparing.

(c) The other purpose of visual material is to entertain. Illustrations especially add to the enjoyment of a publication; prime examples are cartoons and comics. While the visual should pertain to the text in some way, illustrations may be humorous or otherwise add to the entertainment value of the publication. Some graphs and charts may also be used to add entertainment value.

(d) Visual material also helps to break up the text, which makes the publication more inviting to look at.

13.10.2 Range of editorial tasks

Visual materials present a number of challenges for editors. For that reason, visual materials may seem daunting.

(a) First and foremost is consistency and correctness. If many similar visuals appear in a publication, the editor should check that they are presented in a consistent manner and that the information they convey is accurate.

(b) Perhaps the most important editorial considerations are the purpose of the visual material and the intended audience. In some cases, visual material is expected, or even necessary; for example, a children's picture book requires illustrations. The editor must also consider the audience when determining the appropriateness of visual material.

(c) The other major consideration is the purpose of the visual material in the text. Extraneous or unnecessary visual material distracts the reader and creates clutter on the page.

(d) Formatting may present special challenges. For example, an editor may find it difficult to correct a graph depending on what program was used to generate it. It may also be difficult to impose consistency, especially across several graphs. The editor should also ensure that the graph does not skew information.

Other visuals present similar challenges.

(e) Photographs and reproductions of artwork present a different set of challenges, in that they may need to be cleaned, cropped, or colour-corrected. Text-based visual material is usually the easiest to edit.

(f) For almost all visual material, certain technical requirements must be met. A minimum resolution must usually be met; the resolution is dependent on format (see 13.10.3.2.1). Print requires a higher resolution than electronic publications. Other technical requirements include file formats, the use of layers, and the embedding of fonts.

(g) Editors must also consider legal aspects of including visual material, especially material created by or sourced from third parties. Illustrations may be purchased, while photographs and reproductions of fine art may need to be licensed. Some material may be adapted from a source to better suit the publication's needs. If permission is needed from a third party, the editor may also be responsible for editing and styling credit lines. For visual material that is adapted or draws information from another source, a source line should be included. (For a discussion of seeking permission, see ECE3, 10.3.12.)

(h) Sourcing appropriate visuals and determining placement within a publication may also fall to the editor. When placement is at the editor's discretion, the editor must pick an appropriate place for the visual in relation to the text, and also consider page layout.

(i) If there are references in the text to visuals found elsewhere in the publication (e.g., references in an essay about an artist's work to paintings reproduced at the back of the catalogue), ensure that the text refers to the correct visual and that the format of the references is consistent.

13.10.3 Principles of editing visuals

Visual material can inform and entertain readers, but it must be edited well to perform its function, and there is a wide range of editorial tasks and considerations—almost as numerous as the types of visual material. In the sections that follow, specific concerns and considerations related to editing various types of visual materials are explored in more depth.

13.10.3.1 Basis for editorial decisions

As an editor, you will likely be involved in a number of key decisions about the visuals in a publication. You may provide direction on the visuals to source. You may decide whether the sourced visuals are appropriate, or whether they need to be adjusted in any way. You may proofread the final product. When making editorial decisions, consider the following:

- **Function**: What is the function of the visual in this specific context? Is it meant to illustrate a point from the text adjacent to it? Is it representing a more abstract concept (e.g., a political cartoon)? Is it an infographic meant to explain complex ideas in a visual way? Once you've established the intended function of the visual, consider whether it's doing the job.

- **Audience**: Who is the intended audience of this publication? Is the visual appropriate for this audience?

- **Quality**: Are the chosen visuals the right quality? Are they the right size, colour, and format? Do they match the nature of the publication (e.g., do the visuals look like the work of an amateur when you're striving for a more professional presentation)?

- **Content**: Is all of the information that needs to be in the visual displaying correctly? Did part of the visual get cropped accidentally? If the visual contains text, is any part of the text missing or unreadable? Does the information in that infographic make logical sense?

- **Style Guide**: Many publishers and organizations have a style guide that covers not only grammar and preferred spelling but also visual identity—dictating the appropriate use of visuals, fonts, logos, corporate colours, headings, captions, etc., across a variety of communication platforms. Use the style guide as your main reference point. If your organization does not have a style guide, consider creating one for the publication you're working on.

- Also refer to the style guide when editing text within visuals. Treat the text in an infographic or illustration the same way that you would treat text in the rest of the publication: proofread it carefully! You'll be surprised at how often spelling mistakes creep in.

13.10.3.2 Technical considerations

In a digital world, the most important technical considerations for ensuring high-quality visuals are resolution (dpi), image size, and colour. Talk to your printer or production manager when in doubt, and before submitting any final artwork. They will tell you everything you need to know, and help you avoid common pitfalls.

13.10.3.2.1 Resolution

(a) For print publications, you want to ensure high resolution for a sharp image. This usually means 300 dots per inch (dpi) at the size you plan to print the image. For example, if you're printing a photograph at 3 by 5 inches, you want the digital file to be 3 by 5 inches at 300 dpi. Therefore, when sourcing images, always ask for the highest resolution you will need. You can scale down to produce lower-resolution images for the web, but you can't scale up if you start with a low-resolution image.

(b) When proofreading a print publication, watch for grainy or blurry images—this is usually a sign of low resolution.

(c) For websites, online publications, e-newsletters, and social media, keep the resolution at 72 dpi for faster loading.

13.10.3.2.2 Image size

There are many programs you can use for sizing visuals, including Photoshop, Preview (for Mac users), and Windows Office Picture Manager. Refer to your style guide for image size when treating different elements in your publication (e.g., banner images on a website or e-newsletter, or illustrations in a picture book).

The chart below gives a rough overview about digital file sizes. The specifications are approximate values, which differ slightly from scan to scan.

Chart for determining size

5 MP = 2592 × 1944 pixels High quality: 10 × 13 inches
Acceptable quality: 13 × 19 inches

4 MP = 2272 × 1704 pixels High quality: 9 × 12 inches
Acceptable quality: 12 × 16 inches

3 MP = 2048 × 1536 pixels High quality: 8 × 10 inches
Acceptable quality: 10 × 13 inches

2 MP = 1600 × 1200 pixels High quality: 4 × 6 inches, 5 × 7 inches
Acceptable quality: 8 × 10 inches

For an online inches-to-pixels calculator, visit pixelyzer.com
/inches_to_pixels.html.

13.10.3.2.3 Colour

(a) Working with colour requires a basic understanding of
RGB, CMYK, and PMS. (For more on colour reproduction, see
13.2.1.2.3 and 13.2.1.3.1.) RGB (red, green, blue) colours are used
on computer screens; all images on the web are in RGB. Those
RGB colours are then converted to CMYK or PMS for printing.
CMYK (cyan, magenta, yellow, black), also called four-colour
process, is used on most colour printers. PMS (Pantone Matching
System) involves mixing precise inks to achieve the same result
every time, and requires offset printing. PMS colours are often
used in logos and corporate identity.

(b) When preparing a digital file for printing or for uploading to
the web, make sure the colours are set appropriately. For more
information, talk to your production manager or printer, or visit
the following blog posts:

Creative MediaWorks, "RGB vs. CMYK vs. PMS—Why Doesn't
My Printout Look Like My Screen?": creativemediaworks.com
/White-Papers/?id=1.

VisibleLogic, "CMYK, RGB, PMS: Color Systems Defined": visible
logic.com/blog/2011/05/cmyk-rgb-pms-color-systems-defined.

(c) The important thing to remember is that because RGB
colours used on your computer screen get converted to CMYK

or PMS for printing, it is difficult to match the colour you see on the screen to the printed version. Whenever possible, request a printed proof instead of a digital PDF proof.

13.10.3.2.4 Placement on the page

If the visual is coexisting with text on a page, ensure that it's not too close to the text, and that the text doesn't contain funny spacing, orphans, or widows. If there is text on top of the visual, make sure that it's easy to read. For instance, readability will be compromised if black text appears on a dark image. Consider switching to white text or lightening the image. If the image is in a centrefold, ensure that no important details are being lost to the fold.

13.10.3.2.5 Cosmetics

Sometimes, a visual looks that much better with a bit of Photoshop magic. Most photographs require some form of colour correction to compensate for imperfect shooting conditions. It's therefore helpful to have basic Photoshop skills for correcting skin tones, contrast, and brightness, and for eliminating any distractions (such as a black speck on a white shirt).

13.10.3.2.6 Consistency

(a) Strive for consistency within the publication:

- Keep the visuals at the same level of quality.

- Keep the same types of visuals at the same size.

- Ensure that captions accompanying the visuals are placed in the same spot for each visual, and that the format and the font size of the captions are consistent.

(b) If you're working on a communication campaign with a variety of components, or a print and web version of the same publication, keep your visuals consistent across the platforms. This helps to establish an at-a-glance association between the visuals and your campaign. Remember to adjust the size, colour, and resolution of the visuals to match each medium.

13.10.3.2.7 Legal and moral issues

(a) It is very important to obtain permission for each visual you plan to reproduce in your publication. You can do this in a number of ways.

187

- Purchase the image from a stock photography website such as Dreamstime, iStock, Getty Images, or Flickr. The cost of the image includes the copyright fee. (For a discussion of Creative Commons licences, see ECE3, 10.3.12.4.)

- Obtain permission from the owner of the image (see ECE3, 10.3.12). For example, if you find an image on another website and it includes contact information, get in touch with the owner; describe the context in which you want to use the image, and ask for permission. You may be surprised—permission may be granted without having to pay a fee.

(b) Where appropriate, credit your source (e.g., Getty Images, or the name of the photographer).

(c) If you are taking photographs yourself, obtain legal consent from any subjects you plan to photograph. (For a discussion of model releases, see ECE3, 10.3.11.)

13.10.4 Text considerations related to visuals

Visuals can add depth and beauty to text or be sources of frustration and annoyance that leave readers baffled. Proper titles, captions, or labels can make all the difference. If you are working on a publication (whether print or electronic) that includes visuals, you will have to deal with these text-related aspects. Before you start, as with all editorial tasks, know your responsibilities. Check with the publisher on what the author is supposed to do versus what you're supposed to do—and what will happen if the author doesn't come through (e.g., you have to write captions and specify labels). If you're working with a self-publishing author, check what she or he plans to do about items like captions and labels. If nothing is planned, you may need to provide guidance.

Know what the publisher's style is for titles, captions, and labels for the particular publication you're working on. Don't assume anything. Not every publisher follows conventional styles (e.g., some prefer figure numbers and captions above visuals, whereas typically they're placed below). The house style guide should include information about text related to visuals, just as it does for other text elements such as head levels and punctuation. If it doesn't and your manuscript includes lots of visuals with text-related elements, write your own style guide. As in all things editorial, consistency is what we strive for—though it's not always completely achievable.

13.10.4.1 Titles

(a) Titles appear above visuals. They are typical of tables, graphs, and charts but much less common with photos and art. As with all visuals-connected text, titles should be informative but not too long. For example, a photo of a beach at sunset isn't enhanced by the title "Sunset." Making it "Sunset at Long Beach" at least puts the reader in the right place.

(b) Table titles usually include a number so the table can be easily referenced in the main text. Don't include the numbers in table titles until you know their exact order in the final document. Otherwise, you may end up renumbering them with every new draft.

(c) Graphs are unique in that they may include both a title above and a caption below. The title above indicates what is plotted on the graph (e.g., "Speed vs. Time") while the caption below provides some interpretation or explanation (e.g., "This graph shows speed changing at a uniform rate."). In academic and educational publishing, the title/caption combination for graphs is usually required. In trade publications and magazines, this is less common.

13.10.4.2 Captions

(a) Captions can vary from just a number to a paragraph or more in a photo essay. More commonly, they are a brief description of what is in the visual—just long enough that readers know what they're seeing. Captions may be used just as an identifier (e.g., "Figure 3.2 Cross-section of a volcano") or provide explanatory information about the visual (e.g., "Victoria's cherry trees were planted in the 1930s."). Captions shouldn't simply repeat what's in the text, but they should use consistent terminology and should never contradict information in the text.

(b) In some cases, captions must include credits for the originator of the image. Make sure you know how these are supposed to appear; some sources require very specific wording. (See 13.10.3.2.7.)

(c) Captions should not seem random—appearing with some visuals but not others. The consistent use of captions helps readers understand the content and guides them through the text. If text referencing is important (i.e., the visual must be referenced in the text), figure numbers are essential. Figure numbers also prevent the awkward "see photo above" or "see photo below" indicators, which don't work well with some electronic or online documents. As with tables, don't add the figure numbers until you are sure of the final order in which the visuals will appear. Renumbering can seem endless after several drafts and creates opportunities for errors.

For more information about captions, visit the following websites:

"Captions," *Wikipedia Manual of Style*, en.wikipedia.org/wiki /Wikipedia:Manual_of_Style/Captions.

Malcolm Gibson, "Photo Captions and Cutlines," *Wonderful World of Words*, web.ku.edu/~edit/captions.html.

13.10.4.3 Labels

(a) Labels are informative bits of text that appear on diagrams, graphs, charts, maps, illustrations, photos, and any other kind of visual. Their purpose is to identify specific features in the image. But they can be tricky. They have to be clearly worded, informative but concise, consistent in appearance and wording within the visual and with other visuals in the publication, and large enough to read without obscuring the important parts of the image. Labels on a diagram that instructs how to assemble a chair should identify each of the parts and possibly also include arrows pointing to what fits where. In graphs, the x-axis and y-axis must be labelled so graphic information can be interpreted. But graphs often include other labels as well (e.g., indicating interesting areas or a particular point or points). Other types of visuals, such as maps, also have specific requirements for labels. (For more on maps, see 13.10.5.6.)

(b) Length and size of labels are important considerations. Keep in mind that if a visual with labels is resized, the labels will have to be adjusted—shrinking a visual may make the labels so tiny as to be unreadable; enlarging the visual could make the labels look incongruously large. In the design process, it's best if labels are kept separate from the rest of the image so they can be easily adjusted. This is also helpful if the visual will be produced in French, as wording in French tends to be longer than in English.

(c) Another issue with labels can occur when a visual is picked up from another source. Do you adjust the labels to the same style as in other visuals in your publication, or do you leave them as is? This may not be a question at all if the copyright owner won't allow changes. If changes are permitted, use the opportunity to ensure consistency in style both within the visual and with others and to improve clarity, if needed.

(d) For electronic publishing, check how the labels will look onscreen in different browsers and platforms. Do they stay in the right place? Is the font clear?

13.10.4.4 *Text seen as visuals*

Sometimes text has a bigger role to play than just conveying information. Of course, all designers want to use attractive fonts, but sometimes text is an important design element. In a graphic novel, hand-lettered text helps to express the artistic vision of the author. In a history book, a "handwritten" letter may add authenticity to the main text.

If the text is meant to be read and understood, as well as being visually distinctive, your role as editor is important in help- ing to balance design with readability. Consider factors such as colours, busyness of background, size of text, and font style. Sometimes what looks attractive at the outset doesn't work in a specific application. For example, in a textbook in which worked example problems are done in a typeface that supposedly mim- ics student hand printing, the numbers may prove difficult to make out in fraction format because of the shapes of some of them (e.g., the curve on the tail of the "9").

Other aspects to pay attention to are unusual indents and irregu- lar margins. As with all editing, think of the reader.

13.10.5 Types of visual components

There are often a variety of visual components within a project, such as line drawings, paintings, photographs, charts, graphs, maps, and illustrations. Visual components should be numbered uniquely in the art log to ensure that the correct visual is placed during the production stage. This is particularly essential when handling a large number of visuals within a project.

13.10.5.1 Lists

(a) Lists are useful, as they break overly long sentences into information chunks that are easier to digest.

(b) Use unordered (bulleted) lists when the information does not need to be in a particular order.

(c) Use ordered (numbered) lists when the information is in a particular order or it refers to list items by number (e.g., steps of a procedure, items on a checklist, requirements in a specification):

(d) Sometimes lists can be too long and require additional organization. This can be achieved by subdividing the list, if possible:

Fruit
    Apples
    Bananas
    Blueberries
Meat
    Beef
    Chicken
    Pork
Vegetables
    Carrots
    Kale
    Spinach

13.10.5.2 Charts and graphs

(a) Charts and graphs are visual tools to explain concepts using data. They are used to make data more effective, interesting, and easy to understand. The right graph or chart is a powerful tool to present data in a logical and consistent manner.

(b) Charts are usually interpreted more easily than the raw data that they are produced from. Certain types of charts are more useful for presenting a given data set than others. For example, line graphs are used to track changes over short and long periods of time. Pie charts are used when comparing parts of a whole and do not show changes over time. Scatter, or bubble, charts show the relationship between two or more variables and how they relate to one another.

(c) In most cases, data is not covered under copyright. However, permission is needed for more complicated charts and graphs, such as infographics, in which data is not just presented but analyzed.

(d) The chart title should accurately describe what the chart is meant to depict. It should be large enough to be readable but not so large that it is distracting. The legend describes the data. The colours of the items within the legend should correspond to the data on the chart. Designers are usually tasked with finding creative ways to display charted data to make them visually appealing but also to make the chart or graph easy to interpret.

For more information about types of charts and graphs, visit

Andrew Abela, "Chart Suggestions—A Thought-Starter," *Extreme Presentation*, extremepresentation.com/uploads/images /choosing_a_good_chart.jpg.

13.10.5.3 Photographs

(a) Photographs can be sourced through a variety of repositories such as Library and Archives Canada, the Library of Congress, Canadian and U.S. government sources, university libraries, NGOs, corporations, museums, micro stock agencies, specialty stock agencies, illustration sources, photographers, and photographer collectives.

(b) The budget for the project may often dictate the source of images. However, do not automatically assume that a stock agency photograph or one from a famous photographer will be too expensive to use. Submit a query letter to the photographer or stock house with the publication details of the project and ask for a quote. Most stock agencies and photographers are willing to quote on licensing fees.

(c) The advantage of obtaining images through a stock agency is the quick turnaround and the high-quality scans. The reproduction fees for images in the collections of museums and archives are often less expensive than from stock libraries. As well, take into account the time involved in getting images from museums and public archives. Many of them have now digitized their collections and can fill an order for images fairly quickly; however, some are understaffed, and it can take 4 to 6 weeks or longer to receive the high-resolution scans.

(d) Some picture stock agencies specialize in a particular subject area. For example, Bridgeman Images specializes in fine art photography and history, Science Photo Library specializes in images relating to science, and Landov Media and Canadian Press Images specialize in editorial news-related photography. The Picture Archive Council of America (PACA; pacasearch .com) is a good source to search for images and picture agencies.

13.10.5.4 Illustrations

(a) The author's manuscript is usually the first indication the editor receives of the type of artwork that will be needed. Some illustrations can be sourced from agencies specializing in illustrations, but in some cases artwork has to be commissioned from a freelance illustrator or created in-house.

(b) Ideally, the author should supply references or a detailed brief of the type of illustration required. A copy of the text is sometimes sufficient for an illustrator, but additional reference material should be included when necessary. If the illustrator does not understand the concept, he or she cannot visualize and therefore execute the artwork in a timely and accurate manner.

(c) In many cases, freelance illustrators illustrate children's picture books. Often, the editor or publisher chooses an illustrator whose style best suits the text. Picture books are usually 32 pages and contain fewer than 1,000 words to tell a complete story with engaging characters, a compelling plot, and an emotionally resonant theme. Illustrations are an essential component in telling that story, and the illustrator is an equally important creative contributor. Instead of the process being strictly between author and editor, children's books have more key players, specifically the author, editor, illustrator, and art director.

13.10.5.5 Technical illustrations

Technical illustrations generally describe and explain subjects to a non-technical audience. Therefore, visual images should accurately reflect dimensions and proportions and should provide an overall impression of what the object is or does.

Examples of technical illustrations are those found in manuals for automobiles and consumer electronics. These types of technical illustrations contain simple terminology and symbols that can be understood by the layperson. Technical illustrations and graphics are also used in material used by professionals in many fields, including aerospace, military, and electrical engineering. The illustrations may contain complex terminology and specialized symbols. Often these illustrations contain jargon and symbols not understood by the general public.

Types of drawings in technical communication are

- conventional line drawings
- exploded view drawings
- cutaway drawings
- clip art images.

13.10.5.6 Maps

Virtually all maps (except some from U.S. government sources or historical maps that are in the public domain) are subject to copyright, regardless of the source media (print, Internet, CD-ROM, etc.). This is true of street maps and atlases, road maps, decorative maps, perspective view maps, wall maps, locator maps, cartoon maps, and globes. Historical maps can be obtained from archives or from stock agencies that contain historical collections. Permission to use maps should be obtained from the source company.

13.10.5.7 Comics

"Comics" are images and, often, words organized in a sequence to tell a story. Comics may be long or short; "graphic novels" are long-format comics. Graphic novels do not always refer to novels—they include, for example, short story collections and non-fiction books. Since comics are a medium and graphic novels are a format, this section will refer to "comics."

For a concise definition, see Jessica Abel, "What Is a 'Graphic Novel'?," *Drawing Words & Writing Pictures*, Dw-wp.com /resources/what-is-a-graphic-novel. For an in-depth discussion, see Scott McCloud, *Understanding Comics* (New York: HarperCollins, 1993).

13.10.5.7.1 Different types of editing and publishing

Comics take a variety of forms, and different publishers will have different expectations for editors. For example, publishers of franchise comics have clear guidelines for all aspects of artwork, plot, and character development. Publishers of non-franchise comics take a range of approaches. Publishers who understand comics as fine art take a curatorial approach: If they like it, they publish it; if not, they won't. There is little to no editing between acquisition and publication. On the other hand, publishers who understand comics as literature may expect several rounds of structural editing, stylistic editing, copy editing, and proofreading. Both art and words may be edited, depending on the stage of development (see table 13.10.2).

Table 13.5   Editing at different stages of comics development

Stage of comics development		Structural & stylistic editing		Copy editing		Proofreading	
		Art	Words	Art	Words	Art	Words
1	Concept (pitch, outline/story map/beat sheet, character designs)	Yes	Yes	--	--	--	--
2	Script (dialogue, captions, and descriptions of art)	Yes	Yes	--	Yes	--	Yes
	Roughs (minimal-detail page layouts/ thumbnail sketches)	Yes	Yes	--	--	--	--
3	Pencils (detailed final-draft layouts)	Only if neces-sary	Only if neces-sary	Yes	--	--	--
4	Final art (inked, toned, coloured, and lettered)	--	--	--	--	Yes	Yes

As the art progresses from concept sketches, to rough layouts, to detailed layouts ("pencils"), to final art, it becomes increasingly time-consuming and costly to make changes. A good editorial rule of thumb is to catch as many issues as possible at the script and roughs stage.

For further reading

The publishing process: Devin Larson, "Overview of the Comic Creation Process," *Making Comics*, makingcomics.com /2014/01/16/overview-comic-creation-process.

Sample process through scripts, thumbnails, pencils, inks, colouring, and lettering: "Making of a Comic," Dark Horse Comics, darkhorse.com/Features/Making-of-a-Comic.

Annotated comics script page: Nate Piekos, "Comic Script Basics," *Blambot*, blambot.com/articles_script.shtml.

Sample scripts from well-known creators: "Script Archive," *Comics Experience*, comicsexperience.com/scripts.

Canadian companies that publish comics: "Canadian Comic Book Publishers," joeshusterawards.com/links/links-to-canadian-publishing-companies.

13.10.5.7.2 The team

Publishing comics involves a creative team (often, a writer, penciller, inker, toner or colourist, and letterer) and an editorial team (at minimum, an editor and an art director or designer). Often the writer and the penciller will collaborate at the script and roughs stage, editing each other's contributions. Typically, the editor will focus on editing the storyline and character development and the art director will focus on composition and visual flow. However, in comics, the visual elements both structure and pace the story. Pictures are not illustrations but rather an inextricable part of the text. As a result, the lines separating editorial and art directorial responsibilities are blurry and shifting. The editor and the art director (or designer) must work collaboratively and coordinate their feedback to the creators.

13.10.5.7.3 Page flow

English-language comics are typically read left to right, top to bottom. Japanese-language comics flow right to left, top to bottom. Each visual element—lines, angles, shading, colours, panel frames, speech balloons, etc.—plays a role in guiding the eye across the page and communicating the story. An editor should not edit panel by panel but rather page by page, or double-page spread by double-page spread. It is a good practice (though not a rule) to end on a strong note in the last panel of each recto page. This may be a compelling image, a cliffhanger moment, a question, or a teaser of some kind.

13.10.5.7.4 The safe area and the bleed

It is important for the artist to know the trim size the publisher has set for the publication. Most panels are contained within the "safe area" or "live area," a zone usually set 0.25 to 0.5 inches inside the trim line. At the roughs and pencils stages, editors should ensure that all words are contained within the safe area, along with all other important elements (e.g., faces, hands, clues). The area that extends past the trim line is the "bleed." "Full bleed" panels extend to the edges of the trimmed page, strengthening a panel's visual impact.

For further reading

Details on creating layouts and using the bleed: Jessica Abel and Matt Madden, "Layout Quickguides," *Drawing Words & Writing Pictures*, dw-wp.com/resources/cartooning-quickguides /layout-quickguides.

Sample page with standard comic dimensions: Nate Piekos, "Original Art Dimensions for American Standard Comics," *Blambot*, blambot.com/articles_artdimensions.shtml.

13.10.5.7.5 Shots and framing

(a) Shots vary from wide-angle establishing shots, to medium shots, to close-ups, to extreme close-ups. Establishing shots give us the parameters our protagonists are moving in—alien planet or high school classroom or dark and stormy night. They are often found at the top of a page whenever the scene changes. Medium shots show all or part of characters' bodies; they are often used for action sequences or dialogue. Close-ups are usually used to convey emotion.

(b) Shots are typically contained within panel lines; removing one or more of these lines generates additional drama. Likewise, extending artwork into the bleed can have a strong impact. The fewer panels there are, the more visually powerful the page. A dramatic moment of discovery may take place in only one panel spread across two pages. A fight scene usually takes up only three or four panels per page.

(c) At the script and roughs stage, an editor should consider the types of shots and the number of shots per page:

- How many panels are needed to express what is happening? How important is this moment? For example, if the writer or artist has dedicated five panels to close-ups of a character's face moving from happy to sad, is that too many? Does this number of panels overemphasize a small moment or a minor character? Or is this a critical turning point in the story? If so, should it take up the whole page?

- Is the pacing working? Is it going too fast (e.g., the page is crowded with actions and plot developments)? Or is it going too slow (e.g., multiple shots being used to make the same point)? Are there panels that should be expanded into more pages? Are there panels that should be condensed or merged? Make sure that there aren't too many story elements — actions or emotions, dialogue — crammed into a single panel or onto a single page. A character cannot show more than one emotion at a time; therefore, a character's speech balloon should convey only one emotion. If a character is moving from happiness to anger to despair, each of these emotions needs to have its own panel or panels so that the reader can follow the development.

- Is there an engaging variety of shots in each spread, or do the angles and images come across as static? In text-heavy comics, editors should watch for repetitive shots of "talking heads"; look for alternative shots. Examples of commonly used solutions include providing a close-up of an object that helps to tell the story, pulling back to an establishing shot of the location with speech balloons floating above the scene, cutting to a shot of another person watching or listening in, or showing the events being described by the speaker in a flashback panel or an imagined future scenario.

For further reading

Comics vocabulary, types of shots, and communicating through visual elements: Scott McCloud, *Understanding Comics* (New York: HarperCollins, 1993), *Reinventing Comics* (New York: HarperCollins, 2000), and *Making Comics* (New York: HarperCollins, 2006); see also Jessica Abel and Matt Madden, *Drawing Words & Writing Pictures* (New York: First Second, 2008).

Toronto-based comics creator Ty Templeton provides an excellent hands-on series of courses in how to read, design, write, and draw comics: comicbookbootcamp.com.

13.10.5.7.6 Spatial orientation

At the script and roughs stage, the art director (or designer) and the editor should ensure that characters are speaking in a consistent order throughout a given scene. For example, visual confusion is created if panel 1 shows Person A on the left, speaking first, and Person B on the right, speaking second, but then panel 2 shows Person B on the left, speaking first, and Person A on the right, speaking second. A variation—also to be avoided—is a panel sequence with characters who are placed consistently but who trade turns speaking first, so that their speech balloons have crossed tails.

13.10.5.7.7 Captions and word balloons

(a) In some comics, images move the story forward like the unspooling reel of a silent film; in others, text-heavy word balloons fill every available space inside a panel. As in any kind of art, rules exist to guide clarity and understanding; an expert artisan can break these rules to achieve different effects. Most comics aim to have 25 words or fewer per balloon or caption, 50 words or fewer per panel, and three balloons or fewer per panel. Editors should keep in mind that this maximum typically should not be applied to every panel on every page. Editors should also make sure that any descriptive captions add new emphasis or perspective. Descriptions should not simply repeat the information conveyed in the pictures.

(b) Word balloons and captions may be embedded in the artwork at the pencils stage or superimposed on a full page of art at the lettering stage. If embedded, the size and placement cannot change. If an editor makes a late decision to change the wording, the number of letters needs to remain approximately the same.

For further reading

Balloon shapes, lettering traditions, and comics grammar: Nate Piekos, "Comic Book Grammar and Tradition," *Blambot,* blambot.com/articles_grammar.shtml.

Dark Horse Comics script submission format guide: "Script Format and Specifications," images.darkhorse.com/darkhorse 08/company/submissions/DHScriptFormatGuides.pdf.

13.10.5.7.8 Copy editing and proofreading

(a) Copy editing comics involves the same tasks as copy editing any other kind of prose. You will still make the usual decisions about clarity, conciseness, and consistency, but now they will involve visual elements as well as textual ones. Your style sheet should contain both visual and textual conventions—this is what character X looks like, this is what her car looks like, and so on, as well as the usual concerns about spelling, usage, and numbers.

(b) The words should be copy edited at the script stage; the art should be copy edited at the pencils stage. If the artist produces roughs that are fairly detailed, the editor may do a preliminary check for consistency among repeated elements at that stage. Key questions to ask during a visual copy edit:

- Are all the backgrounds and settings the same? For example, if there is an oak tree in the front yard on page 1, is it still there on page 60? Or is it now a pine tree?

- Are the characters' accessories illustrated consistently? For example, if the character is wearing a wedding ring in panel 1, is it still there in panel 2? Does a character's headgear look like a fedora on one page and a Tilley hat on the next?

(c) Keep a list of elements that repeat. This style sheet should be used to do a visual proofread at the final art stage. It can be difficult and costly to make changes at the final art stage; an editor should make sure that all revisions have been completed before an artist begins inking. Using the two examples above, a wedding ring may be added in fairly easily, but changing the pine tree to an oak tree would be prohibitively expensive.

13.10.5.8 Logos, corporate fonts, and corporate colours

Many organizations have a style guide that outlines the appropriate use of their logos, corporate fonts, and corporate colours. When editing elements of corporate identity, consider the following:

- Is the size of the logo appropriate? Is it too small, making any text in the logo unreadable? Or is it too big, overtaking the other important information on the page?

- Is there enough spacing on all sides of the logo—between the logo and the margins, between the logo and any adjacent text or visuals?

- Is the colour of the logo accurate? Most logos have specific colour values (CMYK or PMS)—be sure to provide these values to the printer.

- Do the corporate fonts appear correctly? Sometimes, fonts can get substituted automatically by a design program or by scripts on a web page or e-newsletter. For easy proofreading, print the digital files.

Editing Canadian English, 3rd edition
More Than Meets the Eh

Revised and updated
Prepared for the Editors' Association of Canada

Editing Canadian English is a style guide, reference manual,
judgment-call coach, and much more. Written by expert editors from
across the country, it presents a flexible but systematic approach
to creating workable Canadian styles.

This comprehensive update includes valuable information on

- Canadianization
- inclusivity
- spelling
- compounds and hyphens
- capitalization
- abbreviations
- punctuation
- measurements
- citation
- the editor's legal and ethical responsibilities
- working with French in an English text
- professional editorial standards

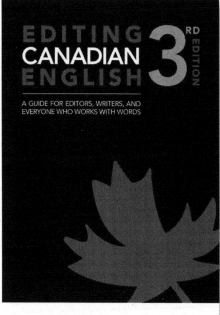

It is an indispensable tool for editors, writers, translators,
journalists, students, teachers, librarians, copywriters,
and marketing and communications professionals
—in short, for anyone who uses Canadian English.

Available as a printed book or an e-book.